Smile Like A Saint. Curse Like A Sailor.
A Guide to Being One Classy Bitch.

By Jennie Hoffer

This book is for all my bitches.
You know who you are.

Insert Sappy Bullshit

A BITCHES GUIDE TO BEING CLASSY

Fake it until you make it.

Always be the heels, never be the doormat.

Own it.

When in doubt, throw it out.

Potlucks & un-friending.

Sisters before misters.

Floss.

Come in like a wrecking ball.

Be a goal digger.

"fuck em, fuck em, fuck em, fuck em."

Don't go hungry.

Be fantastic.

Thirty: The New *"Oh Fuck."*

All of a sudden I realized that the ever popular "in my twenties" did not apply to me anymore. It was as though on the eve of my thirtieth birthday a bearded man crept into my room and took away all of my freedom and excuses. He slapped me across the jaw and told me to grow the fuck up. Jerk. For so long I was able to excuse my shitty behavior with my favorite phrase.

"I don't have a drinking problem! I am in my twenties."

"I don't have a career, I have a job! I am only in my twenties."

"I don't need to think about 401K, unless we talking about dollars. I am in my twenties."

"Hey Amanda! Let's go bar crawling. We are in our twenties."

Then one day I woke up and I was in my thirties. My overused phrase and all the freedom attached to it were ripped away from me. With the passing of one day, I had gone from a free-floating kid to a grown up. I had to start taking life seriously. There is nothing cute about a thirty year old with a drinking problem and serious lack of ambition.

At first I tried to convince myself that I was *only* thirty and I was doing just fine because I was still young. That is until assholes like Mark Zuckerberg go and start multibillion dollar companies in their twenties. Dammit. My twenties were supposed to be my decade of fun and irresponsibility. I was completely unaware of the strings that were attached.

At thirty years old and 14 days, I had to put on my serious face. I had me a soul intervention. I had to sit my ass down and ask myself some very tough questions. *Where am I? Where am I going? How am I getting there? And who is coming with me?* I had to cut myself off. It was a last call for bullshit. If I wanted to do anything worth talking about it would have to happen now. The reality of my twenties was that I had spent most of my time wandering around while working mediocre jobs that ultimately made a few people very wealthy; myself not included. This third decade could not be the same story. That story was not working for me.

One of my biggest issues was my inability to make a decision. I spent much of my time dreaming up grandiose plans while living a completely different life. It was as though I knew I wanted to be something awesome but I forgot about one minor detail. I had to start being awesome. I spent a lot of time planning this amazing journey without bothering to take the first step. Oops. I managed to fly beneath the radar of ambition and coast quietly into my thirties without so much as a plan. That lack of a plan turned out to be just as bad as a shitty plan. A couple weeks after I turned thirty and the nostalgia of it all had faded away, something incredible happened. It was like someone hit me over the head with a frying pan and awakened all of my senses. They say that we live two lives and the second one starts when we realize we only have one life. I had to get to work. I had a lot of shit I wanted to accomplish in my life and this whole mediocre expectation thing wasn't going to cut it. I finally made a decision. I was going to be the best version of me that I could possibly be.

At the time of this soul intervention, I was a Realtor. I was good at it. I probably could have been great at it if I had put any energy into it. The truth is that the occupation itself excited me about as much as a bowl of cashews. I began to dissect the job. What did I like about the job? What did I hate about the job? When I pulled it apart like the layers of an onion, I realized the one thing I really enjoyed about Real Estate was the marketing. And to dissect that even further, I loved writing the marketing pieces. My favorite thing to do was to create clever little mailers about the home I had just sold. My second favorite thing to do was write witty blogs about the assholes I dealt with in Real Estate. I had people reading my blogs from all over the world without any intention of ever using me as a Realtor, but they sure did get a kick out of my anecdotes.

This is when I made the decision. I wanted to write a book. Ahem. I was *going* to write a book. Shit. Make that *books*. I didn't care what it would take and what it would get me; I was going to do it. I had always wanted to write a book but the fire under my ass was never hot enough. Thirty turned up the heat. Once I decided, it was easy. Everything started to make sense and I felt like I was walking the right path. You are currently reading the words of my path. Riddled with profanity it may be, but better here in this book than somewhere they don't belong. Like in a fucking school yard or a god damn grocery store.

"Please: Do everything you possibly can in one lifetime." –Kanye West

As I moved along on my path, I had to take some serious time and review my twenties. I would usually associate "serious time" with drinking but this particular task is best done sober. In order to successfully move forward in my journey and into the next decade with gusto and mental caffeination, I needed to go back and deconstruct my twenties. I needed to decide what baggage was coming with me and what baggage I was leaving behind. The baggage coming with me held all the lessons I had learned along my way. The baggage I was leaving behind held all the reasons I hadn't lived the best version of myself. Everybody has baggage. Baggage isn't a bad thing. However, carrying around baggage that you don't need *is* a bad thing. It is exhausting and tiring and it wastes energy that could be used to make something beautiful happen in your life.

I came to the understanding that our twenties are designed to be a time where we accumulate baggage. It is a time where we are allowed to act a hot mess. It is a time to learn lessons like "don't drink and text." It is a time to makeup and breakup and makeup again. It is a time to discover that humans can function on three hours of sleep. It is a time of irresponsibility and carelessness. All of this is okay and encouraged as long as you can look back, gather all the lessons that you acquired, and apply them to your next decade. What are we but a collection of experiences and memories traveling along a path of decisions and choices? The real challenge is packing for the journey.

You are now entering the Deconstruction Zone. As I transport myself back in time, I give myself a starting point of when I was 20. I had some grand plans. I wanted to be an actress. Cute, right? My parents actually let me drop out of college and pursue my dream of becoming an actress. They even sent me to acting classes and paid for me to get headshots. I still don't know if I wanted to be famous or if I really liked to act, but I guess it doesn't matter since I never made it past audition number one. I went through acting class and was sent to my first audition. Apparently, my skin was not thick enough for the acting industry because at the first criticism, my soul shattered and I never went to another audition. Was I the next Meryl Streep? Hell no. Was my name destined for the big screen? Doubtful. But I look back at that and I am disappointed that I was paralyzed by fear. Fear of being criticized and fear of failing. I look back and I have to question "what if…" I can honestly say that most of my twenties were paralyzed by fear in some form or another.

At 21, I was diagnosed with Anxiety and Panic disorder and put on three different medications. Sounds like a party, right? I became a walking zombie. I remember I got fired from a job I had as an Administrative Assistant or some shit and I didn't cry. I didn't even flinch. I might have even laughed. I watched Titanic and didn't cry. I was so fucking medicated I could have passed as a cadaver. After realizing this wasn't a good look on me, I quit the medicine cold turkey. Hey, by the way, don't do this. I went through a few weeks of hallucinations and mental instability when I did that. Apparently you are supposed to wean off. Oops. I've always been impatient. The good news is that I got off of the medications. The bad news is that I was not cured of my Anxiety and Panic Disorder. Don't worry. I'm a doctor. I can treat this. There is nothing that Coors Light can't fix! And here marks the start of self-medication and a fattening dependency on alcohol. I would not by any measure of the imagination say I was an alcoholic. I would say that I drank every night to alleviate the anxiety I could not control. I had yet to come up with an effective way to manage my panic so beer was the easiest solution. It worked with a few side effects. I gained 30 pounds in about 6 months. Apparently alcohol is fattening as hell. Drinking also causes these little things called hangovers. Hangovers cause this little thing called anxiety. My brilliant little plan to alleviate my anxiety completely backfired. It was time to go to Plan C. Coincidentally, my plan C was all about CONTROL. I had to teach myself how to completely control my environment. Even if I had absolutely no control over my environment and my energy, the illusion that I did was enough to keep my panic and anxiety at bay.

I like to think that everyone goes through some form of panic and anxiety at some point in their life. It's kind of like a long bout of emotional diarrhea. It comes on suddenly and causes pain and discomfort and it fucking stinks and then one day it is gone as though it never happened at all. We can only hope that it causes as little life disturbance as possible and that we come out alive on the other end. The good news is that as with diarrhea, anxiety does not last forever and it clears up in time. Oftentimes, it is simply about weathering the shit storm.

Since most cases of panic are associated with an event or life circumstance, it makes it a bit easier to manage. For example, a person might be standing under the cloud of anxiety when going through a divorce or a breakup. The good news is that if one can cope with the origin, the anxiety will also lighten. The cloud eventually passes. Although this is a comforting thought, the brain does not function on this level when standing under the cloud in the pouring rain with no umbrella. It is hard to remember the sunshine.

While some turn to pills or medication to try and find their sunshine, I violently shake you by the shoulders and vote no. In the middle of the shit storm, taking a moment to recognize the lesson and find the strength deep inside your soul is the greatest fete a human can accomplish. Medication numbs the mind, causes zombie like tendencies and therefore does not cure the problem. After 3 years on medication, I woke up three years older and with the same fucking problems as when I started. Instead of sunshine,

I woke up to all of my problems patiently waiting for me like a beastly 645 pound woman with hairy arms and a tapping foot.

The form of anxiety that I struggled with was a bit more complicated because it had no specific origin. Meaning I had no major life circumstance that caused the disorder, it was just described as a chemical imbalance. That doesn't sound very fucking sexy. The type of anxiety I had would cause me to be in line at the bank and get such an intense panic attack that I would have to leave the bank. I had such an intense feeling of doom and fear that I had to escape the bank and flee to the safety of my car thirty feet away. I can assure you that the origin of my fear was not the teller at Wells Fargo. *Shout out to the banks with drive-thru ATM's.* It was this unpredictability and mysterious origination that made my disorder even more debilitating. I suppose I could have easily said that I didn't know the origin and anxiety must have handpicked me and I could gawk at the random nature of the disease. I could have just popped some pills and been on my merry way. Truth is there wasn't *one* origin. There was probably 4 or 5. I was scared of everything and nothing all at the same time. In everything I did I operated at an anxiety level of 10. I was scared people wouldn't like me, I was scared I would never fall in love, I was scared my car would swerve off the bridge, I was scared the food I was eating would give me food poisoning, I was scared that I had Lupus. I was scared stupid. *Shout out to Google for being my biggest enabler.*

I have spent the last eight years un-medicated and constantly learning to manage my disorder. I have vowed to never pop another pill for my anxiety and never drink another beer to cure this super unsexy chemical imbalance. *Disclaimer: I still drink beer but no longer for the purpose of soothing my anxiety. Now it is because I like the taste of shitty beer.* I have learned that control is the best plan for me. I have come to understand that **fear is energy**. That is it. It is a heart racing, stomach churning, and palm sweating *energy*. It is an abundance of a terrible feeling. So here comes the most beautiful thing about fear. If you can learn to transform the energy from fear into a different emotion, you are able to create an abundance of something else. You can turn fear into something like happiness or ambition or motivation or creativity. In some ways, if you are burdened with overwhelming anxiety or fear, you have an advantage that other people do not. Your body has the ability to create an excessive amount of energy or emotion. All you have to do is train your body to control that energy in a productive way. It sounds about as easy as skinning a unicorn but once you have mastered the skill, you have transformed your life. People always ask me how much coffee I have had because I am so damn hyper. Most times, I haven't had one ounce of caffeine. I am simply taking all the anxiety and nervous energy inside of me and converting it into natural caffeine. I am harnessing the beast! I operate at a level 10, but instead of a level 10 of anxiety, it is a level 10 of excitement. It is a level 10 of ambition. I am a level 10 badass. Same shit, different shape.

There is so much freedom that comes from the elimination of fear. I didn't realize the leash that fear had on my life. When I removed fear from the equation, it completely changed the answer. In my twenties, all of my hopes and dreams were based on accommodating my fears. As I move along my thirties, I do not want to allow my panic and anxiety to handicap me. Like they say here in Texas, worry is like an old man in a rocking chair. It keeps him busy but he don't go nowhere. Amen.

Fear: check. What other baggage did I want to leave in my twenties? What other lessons did I want to bring with me into my thirties? I was about to embark on a big journey and I did not have room for excess baggage and I didn't have time for bullshit. Introducing... **The List**. I spent at least 10 months compiling The List. The List is a collection of all the lessons I learned in my twenties and all the golden nuggets I need to remember as I move along my thirties. The List is my baggage and it is fucking Luis Vuitton. I can honestly say that when making any important life decision, I refer to The List. Before I purchase a new laundry detergent I refer to The List. It keeps me in check and in line with all that I value and all that is important: Being a Classy Bitch.

The following paragraph must be read with a British accent and your chin pointed to the sky.

So here forth and here unto thou who art of awesome descent, upon you I bestow The List for which you are to build your life upon. You are to follow all of these commands as though they are delivered by the Gods. You are to refer to them in times of peril and times of trouble. You are to celebrate when a victory is won and credit here due. You are on your way, and to that I say Cheers you classy bitch you...

THE LIST

#1: Fake It Until You Make It...

There is a reason I have this as number one on The List. As a matter of fact, go shag ass to the closest tattoo shop and have this forever embroidered onto your epidermis. Not as a tramp stamp because then you can't read it. Tattoo this some place where you can refer to it on the daily. Put it in Latin if you want to be clever. I heard white tattoo ink is all the rage. Do that. Just know that this little phrase is the first step in changing your life.

Oh I can already see it now. People are throwing up their arms and bobbling their heads at how horrified they are at the thought of me encouraging women to be phony. Being fake is one of the seven deadly female sins. Number one on the list should be about women being REAL. Women need to embrace who they are and own it. Now simmer the fuck down. I hear you, now hear me. If you read this with shallow intent, any level of shade thrown is happily caught. However, when looked at with a philosophical approach, this exercise is life changing.

There is so much power in what and how we think. It is the most powerful human force. If we can control what and how we think about things, we can change every aspect of our life, both big and small. I get it. It is not easy to change our thoughts. Our thoughts are often wild animals running through our heads as we try our best to tame them. That is why I say start small. *Pretend* you are changing your thoughts. When you look at that person ordering a fruity drink at the bar and you feel your lip go up and the stank eye set in, push out that smile. Force a face. Start acting like your thoughts are changed and eventually your body and mind will follow suit.

When your alarm goes off on a Tuesday morning and the bitterness of life starts seeping in, shake that shit! Convince yourself that you will grab the day by the balls and twist as needed. Your outlook will change the outcome! I can guarantee it. The big question is always WHY? Why must we appear to be okay when we are not? Why must we pretend to be something we are not? Because **the mind is a tricky sonuva bitch and it is the only thing in this entire world that we can control.** Control your thoughts and you can control your reality. You can actually rewire your brain by going through the motions. Fake it and you WILL make it. What you think about, you talk about. What you talk about, you bring about. It all starts with a seed of a thought that grows into a tree called life. Anything you want to be, whether it is healthy, happy, powerful, strong, ambitious, or smart…fake it. Once your thoughts start to shift, the universe starts to shift. Don't believe me? Take your skeptical ass and try it.

Ever woken up and felt like shit? You caught some sort of funky virus and your immune system is on strike, only to realize the minor problem that life doesn't care that you feel like shit. Your boss doesn't care, your kids don't care and your hair don't care. Regardless of how your insides are rotting, you have to get up and get going. As much as you want to lie in bed all day and drug yourself drowsy, tough shit. It is time to begin the chant. "FAKE IT UNTIL YOU MAKE IT." Believe it or not, it is the best medicine you can take. Rather than sit in bed and encourage the illness, get up and show that bug who is boss. Or at least, pretend to show it who is boss. You will be amazed at the results. Sometimes just putting on makeup is enough to make me feel better. It is like a real life mask.

Aside from illness, this mantra also works for the larger things you encounter in life. Take this story about Jessica and Chris as an example…

> *After five long years, Jessica and her high school sweetheart had broken up. It was a tumultuous five years, as most loves are at that young age. Nonetheless, it was her first love. She didn't know anything other than him. Nearly a year after the breakup, Jessica still had not fallen for anyone. She was protecting her heart like it was an endangered species. It wasn't that guys were not pursuing*

her. She practically had a fan club. But she couldn't quite imagine herself with anyone else and nobody seemed to measure up to the man that held her heart the last five years. Although the breakup was a healthy decision, each day that passed built a wall that would be increasingly harder to break down.

To pass the days, Jessica worked at a nice little company right down the street from her house. She had worked there for the past three years and enjoyed the little routine she had made. One Tuesday, a guy knocks on her office door and introduces himself. His name was Chris and he was the new shipping manager. Jessica didn't realize they hired someone. This new hire was very handsome. He had tattoos from head to toe and dressed like he ate cigarettes and spit whiskey. He spoke with a confidence that bordered arrogance and he chain-smoked on his breaks. She was curious, but cautious. The next morning, she caught herself staring at her closet and trying to find herself an exceptionally cute outfit. She convinced herself it had nothing to do with the new guy. He was completely not her type. Besides, her mother would shit herself if she brought this guy home for dinner. Totally wouldn't work. Right?

That day she caught herself strutting rather than walking around the office. She kept finding reasons to go back into the warehouse and speak to the shipping manager. Chris was not even remotely impressed by her. He never even looked up when her heels came clicking behind him. Jessica was used to getting boatloads of attention from males so the fact that Chris didn't pay any mind began to annoy Jessica. That annoyance turned into an attraction and that attraction turned into a determination to win him over. She pulled out all the stops. She was like a peacock walking around with her feathers fanned all day long. Her laughs were getting louder and her skirts were getting shorter.

Finally, after weeks of prancing around like a hungry kitten, Chris casually walks into her office and invites her to a barbecue at his place. She accepts the casual invitation a little too quickly and immediately begins mentally preparing for the evening. This was it. She was going to win him. She was going to make him fall in love with her. Game on.

When she arrived at the barbecue, she was surprised to find that there were only a handful of people there. They all looked the same. They all had tattoos and piercings. They all smoked Camel Lights and wore black converse and drank Pabst Blue Ribbon. Jessica was not like them, but she kind of liked it. As they sat around the fire pit and drank beer, Jessica watched Chris very closely. He was so confident. He was funny. He had a great little bachelor pad and he sure did know how to barbecue. Jessica was undeniably and uncharacteristically falling for him. As his friends slowly started leaving, Jessica stayed. When it came to just the two of them, it happened immediately. He closed the door after the last guest left, walked right over to her, grabbed her by the back of the neck and kissed her like she had never been kissed before. Her knees got weak and her stomach tightened up. It was like something out of a movie. He picked her up off the ground and carried her to the counter. Maybe it was passion or maybe he was the first real man she had experienced. Either way, she liked it. A lot...

She fell fast and hard for the bad boy. The walls she had built came crumbling down. From that point on, she was at his house nearly every weekend and eventually every day. Jessica began to realize why she waited so long to fall in love again. This was how it was supposed to be. Since they worked together, it was of utmost importance that they keep their relationship on the down low. They acted like acquaintances at work and like teenagers behind closed doors. After over a year of being single and mourning her

"Jess. You are kinda freaking me out. Are you sure you're okay? Jared said you were really upset last night."

"Oh, yeah. I definitely had a moment. How embarrassing! Tell Jared I am sorry if he felt awkward! All is well. I am honestly so glad we figured this out in the beginning so I didn't waste another 5 years like I did with my ex. Ya know?"

The look on his face was so fucking priceless that it made all the pain of faking it worth it. Apparently this was not the reaction he expected and he was not pleased. The response from Jessica made it virtually impossible for Chris to reply. She sat there looking at him with a grin and never broke eye contact. She was starting to enjoy this. Everything in her body wanted to cry and crawl over to his feet and beg for his love. She resisted the urge. She faked it. He slowly turned around as if it was his only option left and walked to the warehouse. She spun back around to her computer filled with the most gratifying sense of winning. The feeling was shallow and temporary as the pain of the break up was still lingering deep beneath the surface. But of all the possible outcomes of this moment, this is better than she could have ever anticipated. At the end of the day, she leaves the building and is intercepted by Chris as she is heading to her car.

"Listen. I am sorry. I shouldn't have called you like that. I should've said it to your face. And I should have brought your stuff back instead of Jared. I just thought you were going to be pissed and I didn't want to deal with all that. You were so pissed on the phone. I still love you; I just don't want to get married. I feel like you want to settle down and I still like to have time with my boys."

"Shh. Shh. Stop. It really is okay. And don't worry about calling me. That is what I would expect from you. Might I remind you that you are thirty years old? They are not your boys. They are men. If you started behaving your

six months never happened. She had always been a good actress. She was about to take on her award winning role.

Jessica got out of her car, walked to the front door, looked down at the steps before the entrance and turned it on. When she entered that office, she was not Jessica. She was Jessi-mother fucking-ca. She walked into that office like she owned the place. She happily greeted everyone and sat at her desk with a smile a mile wide. She turned on her music and turned it up nice and loud. She got straight to work and went through her emails at warped speed. When the door to the warehouse opened, her stomach did a back handspring and she felt her heart rate increase with a burst of adrenaline.

"Jessica?" Jessica spins her chair around and smiles at Chris.

"Hey you! What can I do for you?" Chris squishes his eyebrows with concern and squints his eyes in confusion. He apologizes for bothering her and asks her for a purchase order.

"Sure thing. I will email it over. Unless you need me to print it. Is that why you came in here?" He tells her email is good and starts to leave but quickly comes back. They both knew he was there to test her temperament.

"You good? Because I was worried you would be freaking out and having a hard time." She laughed with a flirtatious undertone and assured him she was all good. She even managed to thank him for breaking things off before they got too serious. He leaves. She collapses. But she only allows 15 seconds before she snaps out of it and gets back in the zone. "Stop it you weak little girl." She reprimands herself and carries on with her emails. Then the warehouse door swings open again. Jesus Christ. He was going to make this day a living hell if he didn't stay away from her.

It was over. Even if he came back it was over. The thing about heartbreak is the sobering realization that you knew it all along. Lust is blind. As she laid there on her couch crying softly, she paused. In this brief moment she had the harrowing realization that she would have to face him at work tomorrow. And the next day. And the next. How was she to face this guy that carelessly threw her heart on the floor and casually stomped on it? How could she walk by him in the lunch room when he broke her heart over a phone call in front of an audience? Did he not realize how big of a deal it was for her to give him her heart after all it had been through? Did he not respect the giant, daring leap she took to be with him? The pain of imagining the next few weeks was too much to bear. She decided she would quit. It was much easier than actually facing the music. The horrible, depressing soundtrack of a breakup.

At 5:30am her alarm clock went off. She spent the next 25 minutes trying to find an excuse not to go into work. She was sick. Her car battery was dead. Her heart was deep fried by a tattooed douche bag. No. No, no, no. She balled her hands into fists and grinded her teeth. God damn it. She was not going to let him break her. And even if he does break her, she will not give him the satisfaction of seeing it. Jessica got herself up out of bed and marched to the closet. She dressed in her best Monday outfit and put on her very favorite hoop earrings. She plopped her ass into the seat of her car and jammed out to her favorite music on the way to the office. When she pulled into the parking lot, she stared at the building and began to psych herself out. She talked out loud to herself and cheered herself on. Instead of empowerment, she broke down in tears. It was too much. It was too fresh. How could she be near him and control the urge to hysterically cry? Or kick him directly in his nuts? The only way she was going to make it through the day was to fake it. She would have to pretend like nothing ever happened and fall apart in the comfort of her own home. It was the only way. She had to pretend like the past high school sweetheart, she finally started feeling whole again.

After five months and two weeks of a thrilling and passionate relationship, Chris called Jessica from his friend's phone. She could hear all the boys in the background and could barely understand what he was saying. She plugged her ear and pressed the other tight to the phone as he raised his voice so that she could hear him. "I'm over it. This isn't working for me. You're looking for something and it ain't me."

She stops what she is doing. She replays the sentence in her head over and over again to make sure she is hearing right. Wait, what? She spent the next four minutes pleading with him and insisting that everything was perfect. She said she was sorry he wasn't happy but she could fix it. She begged that they just take a break and talk it out. She pleaded with him to meet with her face to face and talk about things. He cut her off and said he had to go. And then he hung up. That was it. No apologies, no guilt, no remorse. Just a quick phone call to break her heart. After so feverishly protecting herself from this moment, it happened without warning. As she hung up, the world began to spin.

Jessica spent that afternoon in a dizzy haze. She wasn't as upset as she should have been because she was sure he would call her later and everything would be fine. There was no way it was over. Then her doorbell rang. It was not Chris. It was Chris's friend Jared. He was holding a box in his hands. Inside the box was all of Jessica's belongings as well as all the things she had given Chris during their time together. He even returned a barbecue grilling kit...used and covered in black soot. Jared was piss drunk and confessed that Chris was still in love with his ex-girlfriend and they were getting back together to try and work things out. He then admitted all the boys were surprised that Chris even liked Jessica because she wasn't his type at all.

age, you would know that settling down with a female much hotter and younger than you is something to be appreciated. But seriously, thank you for breaking it off. I hadn't realized that our "thing" was probably a rebound and that just isn't fair. So I promise to make work easy and we can carry on as friends. Oh, and best of luck with your ex-girlfriend. She seems like a real catch." She finished him off with a little wink.

And the academy award goes to....Jessica Branson! As much as those words coming out of her mouth were a lie, she knew that in a few months they would be true. It was just a premature conversation. And as she drove away from that parking lot, she felt better. For real better. She did not give him the satisfaction of watching her break. She took all the power away from him. Sure enough, months down the road she realized he was a rebound. She realized Chris had Peter Pan syndrome and would never grow up. He also desperately wanted her back, but that was to be expected.

In every situation, whether it is a break up or some other form of mind fuckery, you have a choice. There is always a choice. You do not choose what happens to you, but you choose how you react. Often times behind Door A is a pity party of one. Choose Door B. Choose empowerment and bad assedness. Choose strength and confidence. It is not the easy choice and therefore the path less chosen. So fake it. Fake it until your ass makes it. Your world will be a better place because *you* decided it to be so.

#2: Always Be The Heels. Never Be The Doormat.

Sometimes you're the hammer and sometimes you're the nail. Sometimes you're the bug and sometimes you're the windshield. Sometimes you're the bird and sometimes you're the statue. It is just the way it goes. Despite all efforts and tantrum throwing, sometimes you lose. While it is completely acceptable to suffer an occasional loss, it is never okay to be a victim. There is a big difference between the two. A loser fights until the bitter end and comes out swinging with two black eyes and growling. A victim lies down and takes the loss while suffering in silence. The loser is wearing heels. The victim is the doormat. The best way to ensure you are never the doormat is to set strong boundaries and standards for yourself. Know when you need to say no. Know when you deserve better than what you are receiving. Make a decision about who you are and what you want and make no compromises. There is no gray area when it comes to your life. It is black and white. You are either winning with a pair of heels on your feet or you are losing with a pair of heels on your feet. No exceptions. The metaphorical significance of heels is dignity. Even if you lose, you are going to make sure you do it with dignity and serving up a fierce dose of fabulous. Losing without your dignity is being the doormat. It is being the victim. It is allowing someone else to decide what you are worth and what you deserve. Oh hell no. You run this ship. Whatever you do and wherever you go, promise yourself that you will never be the doormat. You will never allow someone to walk all over you. If it is happening at work, in your relationship, at school, or in your social life, it is time to get your ass up and put on some heels. Nobody puts baby in the corner and nobody walks all over you.

My creation of this rule does not come without much experience as the doormat. I was a professional doormat. It as is though we must know what it feels like to be walked on in order to understand how important it is to get our ass up. There is a big difference between being loyal and being underappreciated. There is a fine line between being helpful and being overworked. At some point we need to decide if we are going to be walked on or if we are going to walk away. It is at this point that we draw the line in the sand and we set healthy boundaries and high standards. This way we can design our life to happen according to our wildest dreams and without the interference of assholes. We can strut through life wearing our highest heels and we are winning…even when we are not.

This is my story…

For the past decade of my life, I have struggled with addiction. Fortunately, I am not the addict. Unfortunately, I am a bystander to an addict. For over 10 years, I have watched a person that I love very much die every single day. I know that nearly every person reading this can relate to this experience. Whether it is a loved one, friend, family member or acquaintance, each of us has seen an addict get swallowed alive by their personal poison. It is the most heartbreaking and painful disease I have ever witnessed. It is like watching a suicide in slow motion. Anytime an addict has a choice, the drug always wins.

The first couple years were a time of denial. I had convinced myself that there was no way that this person that I loved was snorting chemicals to get high. I had decided it was all a phase and would pass; like acne or voice crackles. I learned to pretend it didn't exist. Ignorance is bliss. I convinced myself the money I gave him was actually for gas and the weight loss was from stress.

It wasn't until the third year that my state of denial was interrupted by the realization of how serious the addiction had become. I could no longer make excuses for the behavior and play along with the games. By that time, it was too late. I had reached my breaking point and this person was already broken. Money was missing from purses, cell phones were gone, and pills were disappearing. The person I had once known was washing away like the sand on the shore. I grasped for the person I used to know and fought for the ghost to return. After several trips to jails, emergency rooms and courtrooms, everyone was exhausted. Loving an addict is about as rewarding as hugging a cactus. It is a constant struggle of trying to desperately save a life and simultaneously prepare for a death. The addict is void of a conscience while those around him are in a constant battle with their own.

Nobody ever has an answer but everyone tries to help. Maybe another therapist. Maybe another rehab. Maybe another hug. Everyone is on the hunt for some magic pill or special treatment center that will finally cure the addict and everything will be as it was once upon a time. The bitter and painful truth is that there is nothing that anyone can do to cure an addict. It is 100% in the hands of the addict. Everyone is always waiting for the addict to hit rock bottom. For a long time, I would throw out the mattress preventing him from getting there. The only thing a bystander can do is control the relationship they have with the addict. There is no pinch hitting and there is no helping hands. Lending a hand to an addict is simply lending a hand to the addiction. What we often perceive as "love" actually loves the addict to death. When an addict is ready, I mean fully committed and ready, they will beat the addiction. It's only a matter of whether or not they can ever make it to that point. They alone have to make that decision.

The addict in my life seemed to enjoy being sick more than he liked being well. Every time he recovered, he would relapse. Sure, this is part of the cycle that we are told to expect. But I came to the realization that my addict liked the cycle. The cycle became his high. It was as though the peace and quiet of sobriety made him uncomfortable so he would create chaos and noise. That was where he was comfortable. It didn't matter what I said, what the family said, what doctors said, what judges said, and what the good Lord above had been trying to tell him during every overdose. He did not see a future free from addiction. The misery and the hustle of a life on drugs were more exhilarating than a life of simple sobriety.

After years of being the doormat to the addiction, I stood up. I decided I would no longer be walked on by this disease. I would no longer be a victim in the situation. For years I had allowed the disease to steal my time, my money, my happiness, and my relationships; all with the noble cause of saving a life. It was almost six years into the addiction that I realized I was ruining my own. That is when I made this commitment. Families and friends of addicts are sadly left vulnerable to the lifestyle and side effects of loving an addict. It is an abusive dynamic. Standing up, setting boundaries, and taking control of your contribution to the addiction are the healthiest and strongest choices you can make for yourself and inevitably, the addict. I decided the addict could kill himself but not me. He could burn his hopes and dreams but not mine. I had to protect myself from being a victim of his addiction. When I did this, it removed all the power that his addiction had over me. It also meant I lost a relationship. Granted, the relationship was with an imaginary person, but it was still a loss. The person I was fighting so hard to get back was gone. Even if he sobered up today, he would not be the person my memory has been holding onto so tightly.

My new strategy in this war has been to be the "heels." I am standing up to the addiction. I decided that I choose what gets my power and energy and I would only give power to his sobriety. I was going to be waiting there when he was ready to live a sober life, but I would not stand by and watch the addiction war. When he was not in recovery, I was not a supporter. For a long time, I would support him regardless of where he was in his fight. Because it was a losing battle that was not my own, I was constantly a victim. So you see, you never fight for an addict and you never fight with an addict. You absolutely and only support the recovery. How egotistical to think that we can cure someone's battle with addiction? How arrogant to think we can beat one of the strongest diseases in the world when we ourselves aren't the person who bears the disease?! Know your boundaries and know where you stand. If you aren't careful, addiction will be standing on you.

This story belongs to so many of us. Maybe instead of pills it is eating. Maybe instead of eating it is physical abuse. Maybe instead of physical abuse it is emotional abuse. We have all been the victim of another person's story. Call it compassion or love or loyalty, but at some point we need to realize what we are losing in return for these things. Stand up.

#3: Own It!

We all have a story. We all have baggage. We all have our chains to break. We all come with a train behind us carrying all our shortcomings, our struggles, our heartaches and our losses. Choo choo mutha fucka. Whether you are the kid with a silver spoon in your mouth or the kid from the streets of the hood, we all have our own threshold for pain and our own story that makes us who we are. Some people start closer to the finish line than others, but that does not determine the winner. Those who start closer might lack the ambition to take the first step. Those who start farther back might sprint past the competition.

It is what we do with what we got that sets apart the winners from the losers. It all comes down to owning it.

"I am 300 pounds and I own it."

"I have a learning disability and I own it."

"I am gay and I own it."

"I am from the hood and I own it."

I know who I am and I am proud of who I am. It is all about quitting the bullshit of trying to rewrite your story or be a victim of your story. It is about telling your story with pride and loving every chapter. You see, society can smell fear and insecurity. I believe it is a simple law of nature. Just as the lion can seek out the weak gazelle and the shark can seek out the weak seal, humans can seek out the insecure human. That insecurity makes them vulnerable to the masses. People can smell that insecurity and they will prey on your weakness. It is no coincidence those who suffer from insecurity often suffer from bullying.

If you are able to flip the switch in your head from hating your story to owning your story, the masses begin to respect your story. They can sense that YOU respect your story. This is the reason that one person and their struggle can be viewed with more compassion and respect than another person with the exact same struggle. It is all a matter of how they own it. "Owning it" can be interpreted as confidence. I think it is a bit bigger than that. Some people feel confident under certain circumstances like when they dress a certain way or have a certain income. "Owning it" is feeling confident when you are broke and in your haggard pajamas. "Owning it" is confidence on another dimension. "Owning it" is a walk and talk that commands respect.

Without a doubt in my mind, *Confidence is more important than intelligence.* Intelligence means nothing if you don't have the confidence to use it. Confidence supersedes any talent and god-given ability.

For the first 20 years of her life, Alana was on a diet. It seemed no matter what she ate and how much she exercised, she sat comfortably at the cusp of obese and clinically overweight. Both of her parents shared the same struggle, but both had seemed to accept what was and carry on without a care in the world. She would watch them enviously as they ate an entire meal without feeling any guilt afterwards. Had she indulged in that meal, she would feel such a heavy burden of guilt that she would spend the next 3 days cloaked in shame and recovering. She hated them for passing on their horrible genetics and for supporting unhealthy eating habits. She blamed them for allowing her to be a chubby kid. She blamed them for not enrolling her in sports to keep her in shape. She blamed society for looking at her with a sideways eye and for laughing at her behind her back. She couldn't even eat in public without feeling like people were watching her every bite.

All of the life experiences that most teenagers looked forward to had left her scarred with memories of embarrassment and self hate. High school prom was a painful parade of unflattering dresses and unavailable sizes. When she finally did find a dress that was suitable, she spent most of prom obsessing about how she looked and wondering if anybody noticed that she could hardly breathe. Every summer was 3 months of pure torture. As the sweltering heat often reached over 100 degrees, she was too ashamed to participate in any water activities, so she spent most of the time sweating in the shade as her friends frolicked in the lake. Even dressing for a normal day of school was a struggle. Most shirts were never long enough and trying to hide the curves of her body was nearly impossible without adding layers and layers of unnecessary clothing.

It was an endless nightmare. It was a day to day walk of shame in her own skin. Everyone always complimented her beauty. Although true, it seemed like a "pity positive" and it was going to take much more to recover her self esteem than a compliment hidden in innuendo. The hurtful words always seemed much louder than the kind ones.

At the age of 19, Alana went to college across town. She was accepted to one of the country's best art schools and was reluctantly excited to start her new journey. Her freshman year started off rocky but picked up around third quarter. She made great new friends from all over the country. It felt like a fresh start. She went out every Thursday to watch karaoke and was hired at a local bagel shop. She was getting into a routine and that made her feel safe. Alana was the opening manager at the bagel shop which meant she had to clock in for work at 4:30am on the weekends. It was a brutal shift but it allowed her to work fulltime and still go to school.

On the morning of Sunday, May 14, Alana was driving to her shift at the bagel shop. As she crossed the intersection in front of the bagel shop, a drunk driver pummeled into her passenger side. She was sent spinning across the intersection and into a light pole.

The next four hours were a hazy blur that ended with her waking up in the Emergency Room. She had IV's going into her arms, machines beeping to her left, and a headache like none she had ever felt before. She opened her eyes to an empty room and began to panic. What had happened? What day was it? Where was her mom? She pushed the red button on the bed and a nurse came rushing in. The nurse quickly checked all the machines and started asking a barrage of questions about the current president and her middle name. Just then a doctor came in with a clipboard. He introduced himself and slowly explained to Alana that she was going to be okay but had suffered a severe concussion, five cracked ribs, a broken collar bone, a left arm full of stitches and staples, and a fractured cheek bone. She filled with fear and started to cry but it hurt enough to make her stop.

A foggy thirty minutes later, Alana's mom showed up. She was crying and hugging Alana and thanking God. She pulled out her phone to show her pictures of her car. Although her mom said it was her car, it didn't look like a vehicle. It looked like a melted crayon with a metal skeleton. The severity of it all began to sink in. Alana had never had a close brush with death. She spent the next four weeks at the hospital; in part because she battled numerous infections on her left arm.

When the hospital finally released her, she was so excited to finally go home. She decided to take a semester off of school and go to stay with her parents as she recovered. Simple tasks like showering and using the bathroom were difficult enough to require assistance. It was a humbling time, but it was a pivotal time. Alana had a lot of time to think. She had a lot of quiet time for reflection. She started a journal to document her journey. Alana was never on her death bed, but coming as close to death as she did on that Sunday morning had changed her in ways she could have never imagined. It was the beginning of a transformation for Alana. It was a time of awakening.

As Alana recovered for those three months at her parents' house, the physical recovery was minor in comparison to the emotional recovery. Alana began to realize the emotional cage she had been living in for the past 19 years. She had been so consumed with how the world saw her that she never looked up to see the world. Although she hadn't died that Sunday morning, she had never really lived the past 19 years either. She thought a lot about the finality of death and imagined her funeral. Who would attend? What would they say in the eulogy? Who would read those words? What impression did she leave on people and the world? She did not like the answers. She realized her work here was not done. Her eulogy was not ready...

She began to discover a new love for herself like never before. She made a promise to never hate herself again. She promised to break the chains that had held her down for so long. She never lost a pound. She never even got on a scale. She decided to love herself exactly the way she was. If it wasn't her weight, it would be her color. If it wasn't her color, it would be her sexuality. If it wasn't one thing, it would be another. The real battle was to love who she was regardless of any of these factors. She decided to own her body; all 245 pounds of it. It was pure freedom.

As the physical wounds healed, so did the lifetime of emotional wounds. She called it her metamorphosis. She decided to stay at her parents' home to enjoy the last of the summer. Part of that enjoyment was going to the lake; the once dreaded lake. Alana could not wait to go swimming. The truth is that Alana had never even purchased a bathing suit. If she ever dared to go swimming it was in a pair of shorts and an oversized tank top. For the first time, Alana went to a store and tried on bathing suits. What she had once feared as a painful activity of embarrassment was something she didn't even think twice about. She walked right into that store and grabbed about 17 bathing suits to try on. She actually enjoyed it. She looked at her enormous boobs and owned them. She looked at her curvy waist and she owned it. The biggest fear she faced that day was leopard print or army green bikini bottoms. She was proud of her body. It was not perfect but the standard for perfect is up for debate.

Alana went with the leopard print. And when she put it on and headed to the shore, she felt like a million dollars. The bikini was a size confident and she rocked it well. For the first time in all her life, she walked onto that beach without fear. She removed her cover-up without shame. She basked in the sun without a care in the world. When she had removed all the cares she had obsessed about in the past, she realized nobody was paying any attention to her. Nobody even cared she was there. All these years she had decided that people would gawk at her and stare at her should she brave the sands of the shore. It was humiliatingly the opposite. When people see a woman who is confident in herself, that is the only thing they notice. It is like a light that shines so bright it is all you can see. Alana could blind an onlooker. Because you see, confidence is like a protective barrier. You cannot hurt someone who is cloaked in confidence.

There is so much freedom in owning your shit. Don't let the opinion of other people become your truth. After all, why in the world would you let someone else own you! That is just plain crazy and I don't subscribe to crazy.

#4: When In Doubt, Throw It Out.

Go ahead. Give that food sitting in that plastic storage container a smell. How does it smell? Questionable? A little funky but you're willing to risk the bout of diarrhea to follow? Fantastic. Now resist all those urges and throw that shit away. It is not worth it. Go get yourself a fresh meal. When in doubt you throw it out. Just as easy as this is applied to your leftover Mexican food, it is also applied to fellow human beings. Dating someone questionable? Throw it out. Friends with someone questionable? Throw it out. It is much better to be sure of the origin than take a chance and risk punishment later. There is a reason you are concerned about that food. Your nose tells you something is a little off and your internal calendar tells you it has been sitting in your fridge for far too long for human consumption. The same rule applies to friends and lovers. There is a reason your senses tell you something is funky about this person. There is a reason you are hesitant to engage with this person. You are smarter than you think when it comes to judging quality. Trust your senses. The diarrhea and the heartbreak are never worth it.

This rule falls under one of my favorite quotes. "When someone shows you who they are, believe them the first time," spoken so elegantly by Maya Angelou and deciphered so eloquently by yours truly. And Oprah. Because if it is deep and insightful you know Oprah already claimed that shit.

Most of the time, people show you how rotten they are from the jump. Or they leave little shitty character crumbs behind. For one reason or another, we decide to take the chance and give them a try. Maybe it is because we enjoy diarrhea or maybe it is because we have really poor judgment when it comes to character. Nonetheless, when they do show you who they are, believe them. If they are rotten, throw them out. Never give someone the opportunity to assault you twice. The second time, you deserve the bruises.

One of the biggest sources of regret in our lives is holding onto something for much too long. How many times have you looked back at a relationship and wished you had ended it sooner? How many times have you looked back and wished you had quit a dead-end job? How many relationships seemed to become more toxic as more time went by? These are all perfect examples of letting something continue to rot when you should have thrown it out. In the end, you are left with wasted time and time is the currency of life. Take that cash serious.

#5: Potlucks & Un-friending.

I love the way social media has softened the emotional blow of disassociating with people. All you do is push a button and VOILA! We aren't friends anymore. Neener neener. Push a button and BOOM! We are in a relationship. XOXO. We don't even have to call people anymore. We let them know that they have been voted off our social island with the click of a mouse. How empowering! And yet, how terrifyingly easy! As simple as it is to remove people from our social media platforms, we should also be incredibly selective in our real life. There is a saying that we are the sum of the five people we hang around the most. If that is the case, you better be holding auditions! You only want the finest and most fabulous specimens in your top five. If you have five awesome people in your circle, you are doing pretty damn well. If you have 3 awesome people and two shitty people, perhaps it is time to unfriend. You are susceptible to being shitty by association. Maybe it is time to go out and make some new friends. If you look around and you are the most awesome person you know, you need to start getting to know more people.

In my twenties is when I came to realize this concept more than ever. I think as a young adult we tend to collect people. We have a lot of friends, a lot of acquaintances and a revolving door of coworkers and bosses. Being that these people inadvertently shape who we are as people, we need to be highly selective of who is allowed to influence our life. I have come up with a great way to "digest" this concept: The Potluck Theory.

Ever been to a potluck? You know; one of those parties where everyone has to bring something that contributes to the meal. Okay. So pretend your life is a potluck. In order to have a successful potluck, all of the attendees need to bring something to the table. In the case of the potluck, you have a variety of attendees and a variety of dishes. You have the people who go above and beyond and bring some homemade main dish that looks like something out of a magazine. You have the people who bring delicious side dishes, usually homemade. You have the people who bring a bag of chips. You have the people who bring a liter of cola. And you have the people who show up empty handed but hungry as hell. Of course there is anyone and everyone in between. In order for a potluck to be successful, you really do require each and every one of these attendees. You have to have a little bit of everything. It's called balance. You cannot have a party full of extravagant main dishes because there would be too much competition and there is no way you could eat that much food. You cannot have a party with forty bags of chips because nobody likes chips that much and they can only hold you over for so long until you become hangry, *a combination or hungry and angry*. You sure as hell can't have a party with a bunch of people who show up with nothing and expect to leave fat and happy. And so is the case with life. You cannot have an imbalance of the people in your life. If your life if full of people who always have to bring the main dish, you are doing okay. Not a lot of variety but an abundance of contribution. If your life is full of people who only bring chips, you have people who don't bring much to the table and try to do things with the least effort possible.

Look at your potluck. How is the turnout? If you find that you have a lot of people who show up empty handed, it's time to reevaluate your attendees. They might be sucking you dry. If you have too many people who bring the minimum to the table, maybe it's time to cancel their invitation. I plan on my potluck being the best damn meal that man ever knew and I want great people who bring great things to the table. Life's a potluck. Eat up.

On the flip side, it's also a good idea to evaluate how you show up for others to their potluck. Are you the person who brings a main dish? Are you the person who brings a bag of chips? You might find that for certain people you are willing to bring the whole fucking turkey and for others you are fine with bringing a package of sporks. That's okay. It's a great way to determine who you value and how you want to show up for them. Make sure the level of importance of someone in your life matches what you bring to their table.

#6: Sisters Before Misters.

Sisters are the best things in the whole wide world. I know this because I have a sister. But don't you worry. If by some twist of fate your mother did not birth you a female sibling, it does not mean you do not have a sister. A sister is your souls best friend; *DNA attachment preferred but not required.* The connection that you have with a sister is stronger than any other connection in the world. When used properly, it can move mountains, it can heal the sick, it can feed the poor and it can mend heartache. Such a powerful relationship should not be overlooked, compromised or underutilized. Having a sister means you never go to a fight alone. It means you never experience loss alone. It means you always have a cheerleader. A sister is like the herpes virus. Once you have one, you have one for life. They will never leave no matter what you do. There might be times when they aren't around, but they are sure to pop up during a stressful or hormonal time to be there for you.

A sister is there to clean up your vomit on your 21st birthday. A sister is there to hold your thigh when you push out a ten pound baby. A sister is there to pee on the hood of some bitches VW when they are mean to you. (*Guilty*) A sister is there to spit on you when you make a bad decision; metaphorically and in some cases physically. A sister is there to call when your friends are not. A sister is there to understand exactly what you are saying in the middle of an unintelligible ugly cry. A sister is there to tell you that bangs were a bad choice. A sister is there to protect you from the super creepy Chewbacca look-alike in the subway. In an ever-changing world, a sister is the only constant.

If you are feeling super bummed that you do not have someone that you can consider a sister, congratulations. This book you are holding can serve as an older sister. This book provides all the advice and ass-kicking motivation that a big sister would provide and perhaps even better. This book is your substitute sister. And in the near future, you should consider finding someone as a soul sister. Hold auditions! There are a few requirements in this person. First, they must be an unconditional friend. No matter what you do or what you say, they remain. This can be a challenge if you tend to be a pain in the ass. A sister doesn't care. They see the core of who you are and the rest is fluid. Second, they are willing to go to bat for you. It doesn't matter who or what the opponent, they suit up and show up for you. Third, they only allow you to be the highest and best you and are damn sure to hold you accountable should you go astray. Whether that means pushing you to do great or preventing you from doing bad, they are getting you to the highest. Treasure this relationship.

#7: Floss.

For those of you unfamiliar with the term "floss," here is the definition according to UrbanDictionary.com:

Floss: to show off or flaunt the merchandise.

I like it. And now here is the definition according to Jennie. To floss is to have your own personal brand. Coca-Cola and Apple have brands for their multi-billion dollar companies so consumers can identify and connect with their company. Their brand is their personality. Just as these corporations have brands, you as a person need to have a brand. To floss is to have a brand that magnifies the best parts of you as a person. It amplifies all the things you love about yourself and it turns them into a character. In order to become a powerhouse, *and that is always the objective*, you need to know how to amplify and capitalize on the best parts of you. When you walk into a room, people should know what to expect because you have a brand. Every powerhouse has a brand. They figured it out that in order to be successful as an individual, you have to floss. Power House Donald Trump knows how to floss. He has a distinct brand that has made him highly successful and internationally recognized. When people hear the name Trump, they know exactly what to expect; a comb over and a bad-ass entrepreneur. Martha Stewart knows how to floss. She built an empire on her best attributes. She became a character and she capitalized on it. These people built a brand as an individual and translated that into an empire with an extraordinary amount of success.

My personal brand is a balance of edgy, cussing, witty, humorous mother and writer. These are all the things I love about myself and have amplified into a character. True success comes when you can capitalize off your personal brand. And there is always a way to capitalize off your brand. It could mean writing, baking, designing, running, eating, whatever! A true entrepreneur knows how to *discover*, *grow*, *create* and *capitalize*. I *discover* my highest and best self, I *grow* it into something larger than anything else in my life, I *create* something tangible, and then I *sell* it. Simply put: find what you are good at and make fucking money off of it. For the first time in history, we have the avenues and technology to think outside the box and build an empire on our own terms.

Empires have been built upon the craziest shit. Tony Hawk built an empire with his passion for skateboarding. Hugh Hefner built an empire with his passion for naked women. Rachael Ray built an empire with her passion for mediocre food. The Kardashians built an empire on being The Kardashians. Judge all you want; an empire is an empire. The Kardashians work hard at their brand. Those are some flossy bitches. And if you think for one second it is because Kim made a sex tape you are wrong. There are millions of sex tapes in the universe and none of those bitches have reached the level of this family. Their success is 100% because of their hard work and ability to floss. Damn. That is inspiring. Write that down.

Also, floss your teeth. Nobody likes shitty gums.

#8: Come In Like A Wrecking Ball.

The first step is to SHOW UP! Once you show up, bring all you have. All that you are and all that you bring to the table needs to enter the room like a wrecking ball. Hold nothing back and leave nothing behind. When you head into that room for an interview, come in like a wrecking ball. When you go on that first date, come in like a wrecking ball. With every entrance you make, you need to imagine fireworks going off behind you and wind blowing in your hair. Imagine the crowd screaming and a spotlight on you while you enter in slow motion. When you leave that board room or that restaurant dinner table, the person opposite you should have their hair blown back and their mustache cinching from the energy and force you just brought to that room. It is better to leave knowing you brought everything to the table than to leave wishing you had brought more.

There are too many times that we come in at 50% because of some underlying fear or insecurity. Fear is the biggest road block in our lives. What a devastating reality. To think of all the opportunities we have lost not because of who we are, but because of what we fear. Coming in like a wrecking ball is an art. It is a practiced form of bad-assery. If you are a wrecking ball, think of fear as the wall.

I will share my life hacks and you can try them out, but I have found that everyone has their own rituals. First, I zone out to music. If I can't empower myself, then I need to call in the troops. The troops consist of Brittney Spears, Adele, Taylor Swift, the usual. Unless you're a thirteen year old girl or share my musical taste, your troops probably look different. That is fantastic. Music is a beautiful noise that drowns out the ugly noise. Use your musical troops to get you in the zone. (That was a Brittney Spears reference in case you aren't awesome enough to notice)

Second, I have a handful of mantras I repeat to myself. Oddly enough, they are the items on this list and a few other noteworthy memes. They are short, sweet and easy to remember when I am preoccupied with nervous energy.

Third, I remember that I do not work in the shit business. I do not give shits and I don't take shit. There is absolutely nothing big enough for me to worry and nobody is important enough to shake me. This might sound like minimizing; I call it real-izing.

Aside from all that, let's be real. It is also really fun to quote Miley Cyrus songs. And we can't stop...

#9: Be a Goal Digger.

In everything you are and in everything you do, be a Goal Digger. Being a Goal Digger means independence. It means strength. It means finding your highest and best use as a human being and going for it. It is ambition. It is refusing to settle and never giving up. It also means you have a goal! Shocking. Sometimes setting the goal is the hardest part of it all. Here I am at thirty two years old and my goals have just now been realized... late but worth the wait! It is amazing the clarity that comes after fucking up.

Once you have decided on THE goal, the rest is digging; relentless, shameless, endless digging. The theory is that if you dig for long enough, you are bound to hit something. Try to focus on digging one hole. Digging several holes is the same amount of work but none of them will get you very far.

Goal Diggers must be warned that with big dreams come big critics. There will be times when people won't believe in you. There will be times when people won't support your goals and possibly even encourage you to abandon your dreams. Don't take it personal. It has nothing to do with you. They are simply trapped inside their own limitations. The ceilings in their head do not allow them to think and dream beyond what is within their reach. Don't let them impress on you.

Because you are a trail blazer and because you are digging where no human has dug before, it is going to be a challenging road. Anything worth it isn't easy and anything easy isn't worth it. You are going to have to be your own biggest cheerleader and you can't rely on others to keep you going. You are your own generator. You cannot plug into someone else and rely on their energy. You do not have a man clapping for you when wake up and giving you a pat on the ass to start your day. You need to be self-sufficient enough to create and survive on your own power. Learn to be your own power source. When shit gets tough, you need to be able to pick your own damn self up and get going.

Being an ambitious human is the best thing you can do for your life. It is what allows us turn a dream into a reality. Ambition is what empowered me to laugh at those who told me I had to decide whether I wanted to be a mother or have a career. Apparently some people believe you cannot be successful at both. Ambition told me I just needed to try harder and try different. Ambition meant I had to give up a little sleep, work a little harder in a shorter period of time, and value each and every free minute that I had. I have a relentless and obsessive determination to succeed that keeps me digging towards that goal until I reach gold. I am always content, but I am never satisfied. So perhaps in some form, I am a Gold Digger.

As I raise my two little boys into men, we talk a lot about their future. I have come to know the importance of your language and wording when you set your goals. I do not allow my kids to say "When I grow up, I want to be a scientist." I make sure that they always say "When I grow up, I am GOING TO BE A SCIENTIST." Make sure that your language speaks directly to your goal. I don't care what you *want*. I want a unicorn. Wanting doesn't mean shit. I want to hear action, not dreams. An action is a dream that has graduated into something that is tangible. You have to start this habit young. It is a pain in the ass to re-learn this concept at the age of 30. Trust.

10: "Fuck em, Fuck em, Fuck em, Fuck em." –Judy Garland

Some time ago I had read an article about the life of Judy Garland. If you don't know who she is, I want you to put down this book, walk to the nearest stainless steel appliance and slam your head into it. Once you regain consciousness, go to your mobile device and Google her. Okay. Welcome back to the world. Your dignity and worth has been restored. This amazing woman with an extraordinary talent and fans across the globe had a ritual that she performed before she would take the stage. When I read about this ritual, I knew she was my kind of lady. She would stand backstage before her grand entrance, and like a beautiful sonnet or psalm, she would say, "Fuck 'em, fuck 'em, fuck 'em, fuck 'em." It was her way of psyching herself out before a performance. At the time I read this, I just admired her for our mutual love of the word fuck. It wasn't until later in my life I realized how much this mantra would help me. Now, I am not a Broadway performer and I don't have any sort of talent that would ever require me to perform. However, anytime that I am about to face a person or a group of people where I am on the spot, I close my eyes and I say, "Fuck em, Fuck em, Fuck em, Fuck em." If it worked for the Queen Judy Garland as she took the stage in front of a massive audience, it could get me through a menial interview with some dipshit broker.

This is not the only way this phrase is useful. If you have a court appearance, close your eyes and chant these eight words before you enter that court room. If you have a presentation to make at work, close your eyes and recite these eight words before entering the board room. If you find yourself wasting time in an argument, chant these eight words. It has this magical way of releasing the fear or the pressure of the situation you are about to face. Some people use the "audience in their underwear" trick to get them through the anxiety. I find this technique to be distracting and sometimes disturbing. The cursing method is far more effective for me. It takes the power away from them and gives it back to me. Ask yourself, who cares? This is not about them. This is about you. What you are about to do is going to be amazing and they can choose whether they like it or not. Bam. Surrender the need to impress these people and instead impress yourself. But when you are reciting this chant, try and keep your voice down. Some people are really fucking weird about the F word.

11. Don't Go Hungry.

Raise your hand if you are guilty of this sin. Now everyone collectively put your hands down because Lord knows each and every one of us has been guilty of being hungry. This is not when we skipped lunch and hit that level of anger only justified by lack of food and plummeting blood sugar. This is that moment in time when we are starving for attention. We become so starved that we behave in filthy and hideous ways to satisfy the craving. You know that drunk girl at the bar acting all sloppy? Hungry. See that loud girl at the restaurant acting all foolish? Starving. It is not a good look and we all know that when we are hungry we behave badly. Remember this the next time you start to hear the belly rumble: there is no need to act a fool to get attention. Act like a lady and get proper attention.

Everyone has a hungry friend. Mine is Nicole. Her hunger is something we have all come to know and accept. If we are going out with Nicole, we have to emotionally prepare for the slew of meltdowns that are about to take place. Poor girl is so hungry for attention that she takes it in any form. Throwing a shoe at the bar is completely standard for Nicole and that is how she satisfies the hunger. Every dirty look, every pair of eyes that gives her a sideways glance and every guy that looks her up and down is a little more hunger satisfaction.

Let's be real. We all have a little Nicole in us once in a while. Completely acceptable. It is usually a result of someone in our life not "feeding" us the attention we crave. Note that when a normal person behaves like Nicole, it is probably under the influence of alcohol and the regret is felt within 24 hours. I am pretty sure Nicole never experienced any shame about her behavior. This, my friends, is a result of a lifetime of attention deprivation and why I never held her hunger against her. Poor thing didn't know any better. She should've been hungry for therapy.

"Seek respect, not attention. It lasts longer."

Mentally, don't go hungry. Physically, don't go hungry. I don't care that you are trying to lose 8 pounds before your trip to Cabo or that your jeans from eighth grade don't fit anymore. You and I both know that starving yourself is going to work for 48 hours at the most and you will be a cranky bitch the whole time. If you want to get it tight, you have to do it right. Hunger in any form is not a good look.

12. Be Fantastic.

The final rule is more of a formula. It is what I call the "Fantastic Five." The Fantastic Five is a group of five people that I admire and idolize for one reason or another. I am not talking about the obvious and cliché answers like my mother or my sister or my favorite teacher. I am talking about famous or infamous human beings that have made an impact on society and my soul. These people tend to be larger than life and that makes it easier to identify their dominant qualities. I have determined that if I group together all the people that I most admire that I could find common denominators of the qualities that attracted me to them. Once I did this, I could determine what I value in people. Take that a step further and I could determine what I want to value in myself. My Fantastic Five was comprised of five famous women who were freakishly alike. They were all very different women with very similar qualities. They were all strong. All independent. All successful Authors. All Comedians. All strong willed and each and every one of them was loud. When I lined these women up, it became very clear that I had a "type." Today, I use this type as a model for how I want to live my life and what kind of person I aspire to be. If I admire women who are independent, successful, loud, and strong, I want to mirror that in myself. If I ever have a decision to make and I am not sure what I should do, I employ the WWFFD method. What would the Fantastic Five do? This method often leads to a decision being ten times fiercer than if I had made the decision on my own. What should I make for dinner? What would Jenny McCarthy make? How should I tell my boss I am going to quit? What would Bethenny Frankel do? It is the best way to ensure every decision you make is in line with the person you envision yourself to be.

This lineup also allows you to take pride in the character traits you already possess. I am what some people call a straight shooter. Sometimes viewed as a negative trait, I often catch flack for this part of my personality. When I look at my Fantastic Five, I realize each and every one of them is a perceived straight shooter. This trait is something I love about them. I have come to realize that this trait is something that I respect in other people. I have come to love and respect this about myself. There were times when people labeled this trait as being a bitch. I used to hate being called a bitch. Now I say thank you.

Build your Fantasy Five. Figure out who influences you and who impresses you. Notice the common qualities that appear in your lineup. Those common qualities speak directly to who you are as a person and who you aspire to be. They serve as a guide for you to understand your own personal definition of success.

Putting It All To Practice:

Now that you have all the rules you need to be a classy bitch and grab your life by the balls, let's put these items to use. These can be applied to any challenge you face; big or small.

Example 1:
You are meeting at the local coffee shop for an interview with a company you would love to work for. The pay is great, the position is perfect and you want it so bad you can taste it! You are

confident that you are qualified; you just need to get past this interview. What do you do?

Refer to #7, 8, 9 and 10. Floss, come in like a wrecking ball, be a goal digger and fuck em, fuck, fuck em, fuck 'em. Congratulations. You're hired.

Example 2:
You make plans to go out with a friend on Friday night. She bails out at the last minute saying she doesn't want to go out so you decide to stay in and make it an early night as well. When you wake up in the morning there are pictures all over her social media of her out on the town with friends all night. What do you do?

Refer to #2, 4, and 5. Always be the heels, never be the doormat. Throw it out. Unfriend. You're good. I know it sounds a bit harsh and kind of like the life version of Survivor but I can assure you. There are amazing and loyal human beings in the world and you would much rather have them along on your journey than shitty human beings taking up space.

Example 3:
You just broke up with your boyfriend of 3 years. Yes, he was a douche and yes you are better off. But changing all your social media statuses and changing your flight status to solo is a bit heartbreaking. What to do?

Refer to #1-12. You will be just fine.

I am sure that I could ~~spend~~ waste a lot of time being angry about my twenties. I could regret the time I wasted and dwell on all the things I could have done. However...

"It is never too late to be who you might have been." –George Eliot

The only tragedy that could take place is leaving behind all the lessons I learned. Instead, I am going to take every lesson and experience and use it as a rocket that propels me into my thirties. I spent the last 10 years attending the University of Life and I am now ready to conquer the world with my baggage in tow. (Throws ceremonial hat in the air) If something dares get in my way, I will take a deep breath and refer to the list. And then pray for the bastard that crosses my path.

I can only imagine how fierce my forties will be…

Facebook is My Space…
And I Am Not Pinterested in being LinkedIn…

"Be aware of the energy you bring into my space."

Wiser words never spoken. This is a favorite quote of the Ms Oprah Winfrey. (Insert applause) Apparently she likes it so much it is on her dressing room wall. Apparently I like it so much it is embedded in my temporal lobe. I quote it on the daily. What it means to me and what it means to you might be a little different but I think we can all appreciate its essence. Basically, when someone walks into the same room as you, what do they do to your energy? What effect do they have on your demeanor? How do you react to their presence? It is said that we as humans have the ability to tap into other people's energy. This energy can also rub off on us the same way that makeup rubs off on someone's shirt when you hug. Don't believe me? Sound a little kooky? I completely agree but read on. How many times have you met someone and for no damn good reason you think to yourself, "There is something off about that fellow?" Or have you ever met someone and the chemistry is INSTANT? These are examples of you picking up on somebody's energy waves, allowing them into your space, and interpreting them in your subconscious. When my son walks into the room, my entire DNA changes. The pitch of my voice changes. My focus immediately shifts. My body language becomes amplified. These same energy changes can be said about him. This is the energy we bring into each other's space. Feel me???

When we think of space, we might think of a room or a house. Or a dressing room if you are the fierce and fabulous Oprah. But nowadays, with the evolution of social media and the world around us engorged in technology, the definition of "space" is more ambiguous and universal than ever. "Space" is now Instagram, Pinterest, Twitter, Google+, whatever. Facebook is now *my space*. Ironic. Once you start viewing social media as your space, you might want to take a look at the energy that is coming into your space. And possibly be a little more protective over your "space."

Social media is a weird ass thing. Can I get an amen? It is still a relatively new concept and I can't even imagine what it will evolve into over the next decade and the next generation. I have always said that we are the guinea pig generation of social media. We will not know for years to come how social media has affected the world around us and how it has transformed the human race. Mark Zuckerberg will be hailed as a heroic innovator or a tyrannical devil in decades to come based on how this all plays out.

My warning to the classy bitches of the universe is to be aware of the capacity of social networking. Exercise caution with every post and every friend. Do not underestimate the power of the platforms. Do not be naive about your social space. There is an illusion of distance but these online communities bring us close enough to smell each other's virtual arm pits. Keep your walls up and your guards on duty. The relationships you are building have more impact on your life than you are aware.

During election time is when I had my first realization of this concept. Anyone who is active on social media knows that times of heightened political activity are when the rats come out of the gutters. I tend to be very neutral when it comes to my political opinions on social media. It is not my soap box and I am pretty sure the chick that graduated High School with me could give a shit less about my stance on gun control. Further, I am not interested in a debate. Your response to my post will not affect my political affiliation, just as the questionably authentic article you posted will have no bearing on my vote at the polls. Plus, have you ever noticed that when people debate from the comfort of a keyboard, the size of their balls is exponential to what they possess in a face to face debate. Yet another adorable side effect of social media in our generation.

During election time is when I found myself becoming very irritated with the HATRED that clogged my feed. Scrolling my news feed I would practically break out in hives with annoyance. Like suddenly the nice lady I knew from work became this arrogant pig at election time. She would post pictures of her adorable Yorkie puppy followed by a hate-laced rant about welfare and liberals. Take it easy pilgrim. You aren't gonna change the world or opinions with your status updates. You are, however, making my eyes roll back into my head for a quick view of my cerebral cortex and for that I salute you with my middle finger. This is when it hit me. She is bringing bad energy into my space. I am getting annoyed by her posts. She is fucking up my moment. It may only be a brief eight seconds that she fucks with, but those are my eight seconds. I can do quite a bit in eight seconds. I can laugh quite a bit in eight seconds. I can drink eight ounces of lukewarm coffee in eight seconds. Without hesitation, I deleted the lady. I removed the toxicity.

It is so important to have an awareness of the energy that people bring into your space. It is important and necessary to set up boundaries in social media. It is important to consider social media as your personal space. GASP! "You mean I should not be friends with anyone and everyone who requests? But she is my coworker's cousin! I want to be informed of all of her daily activities and political views." Yeah. As a rule, if you would not allow them into your home, you should not be connected with them on a personal social media platform. There are some business-related platforms where this rule does not apply. And no, I am not suggesting that all 365 of your Facebook friends come to your house for a tea party. However, each of them individually should be someone you would welcome into your home for an ice cold beer and guacamole. Let's be serious. We are announcing when we are on vacation, we are posting pictures of our kids, we are posting cool new gadgets we just bought, and all sorts of personal shit. We need to have some level of trust with the people we casually connect with on the world wide wizeb.

Furthermore, we need to be somewhat protective of how this massive amount of stimulation and information is affecting our psyche. With access to more information than any other generation before us, we have to wonder the implications it is having on our daily lives. People have said the weather around the globe is becoming more and more extreme and that tragedies are happening more and more frequently. Okay, this is possibly a truth. But I cannot help but wonder if these things always took place, but now we have unscripted access to it within moments of it taking place. Is it really happening more or are we simply becoming more aware? I am pretty confident that Taiwan has suffered many landslides in the past couple centuries, but this is the first time it has had the capability of reaching such a wide audience so quickly. We simply had to click a link and we could learn every aspect of the disaster and view heartbreaking photos of the devastation. And with the simple click of a red heart, we showed our support for the victims. It is with this mind frame that we need to somewhat protect and shield ourselves from the constant and unfiltered flow of information into our lives. While the intention is to bring attention to global causes and create awareness amongst the citizens of the world, I cannot help but think the abundant amount of information is numbing us rather than creating empathy. When we scroll through a feed or social media site, we are inundated with stories purposely created to evoke intense emotion. "Thousands of dolphins slaughtered." "Human trafficking on the rise in India." "Click here if you hope this baby doesn't die of cancer." At some point, we as humans have to put up a wall and turn off our emotional sensory or we would not be able to function on a daily basis. With that, I caution you to protect your space so that you do not become numb to the world around you. More information does not necessarily mean more empathy. Make sure that you monitor the items that come into your world with some sort of filter. I predict the zombification of America in years to come as a result of humans having to shut down their sensors and protect their souls.

Flip the social media coin and we have all the amazing aspects of information overload. I have immense gratitude for all the great energy that social media contributes to my space. I have made some serious and wonderful life changes because of social media. It's like a modern day form of peer pressure! Quitting red meat, nixing vaccinations, jogging routine, teeth whitening. These are all examples of things that happened in my life thanks to social media. I follow a wonderful Doctor on Facebook who opened my eyes to a lot of important health concepts. I started running because some skinny bitch I am friends with inspired me. I whitened my teeth because I found a 75% off coupon for a whitening procedure. You see? Social media has kind of made me a better person…or at least my teeth are whiter. It is all very subliminal. I don't mean to be open to information from that genius doctor or affected by that skinny bitch that runs half marathons, but it happens because they are in my space. I know that if I continue to allow these things into my space that I will continue to have access to opportunity and knowledge. No other generation has had this advantage.

As I shout from the mountaintops preaching my opinion, it all comes down to this: be aware of the energy that you allow into your VIRTUAL space. You might not even realize how it is affecting you. Be protective over your relationships. Control your environment. Be open, but not vulnerable. Be involved, but not annoyed. Be empathetic, but not numbed. Have friends, but don't collect them. And when in doubt, remember that Oprah said so, which means it is Bible. Amen.

D.u.l.i.l.a.h.
Dreadfully Unlucky In Love and Happiness.

She quietly walks into the salon and glances around. She wants to see if she knows anyone in the pedicure chairs. She desperately hopes not since she would hate to be caught parading around town in Ugg boots with no makeup. She is ushered over to a pedicure spa and sets down her Green Straw Cafe Iced Tea and fake Chanel purse. She wished she had brought a magazine but she has her phone with her so she can stalk on Facebook or Perez Hilton to piss the 50 minutes away. When she takes off her Ugg boots she cringes at the site of her poor paws. Not only is the polish chipping away like the Mayan ruins, the spray tan on her feet has created a discoloration on her feet that might mimic impetigo or leprosy. Ugh! Why do spray tans do that? She can't decide if the after effects of the spray tan are worse or the fact that her skin is so white she makes milk look sun burned.

Dulilah sits quietly and snoops around Facebook while the lady paints her toes a fluorescent pink. She has a strong love-hate relationship with Facebook and all of social media for that matter. It seemed as though everyone had this amazing life and did such amazing things, and she was seemingly mediocre. Sure she had a job and was doing all the right things, but Facebook had a way of shining a light on the mediocrity of it all. What the poor girl didn't know or failed to acknowledge is that it was all bullshit anyways. Facebook is the reality show that happens online. It has real elements, but most of it is scripted, forced, and contrived. She spies a photo her friend had posted of her #adorable #newborn and cringes with a cocktail of annoyance and jealousy. Dulilah quickly posts "Getting a pedi! Love having pink toes for a Friday night." Point made.

As she slips the salon-provided flip flops onto her tootsies, she can't decide which are more dreadful, Uggs or fluorescent foam flip flops? She goes with the foam, foreseeing a possible disaster of fuzzy toenails and opting to avoid sacrificing her fresh feet and the $30 she just spent. As she leaves, she contemplates where to go to buy her outfit for the night. She is sure there is absolutely nothing in her walk-in closet. The big challenge is to look cute, but not look like she's trying. Look like she has designer duds, but not look like a knockoff. The process is fucking exhausting. Thankfully, every store in the area caters to the process. She goes to a local store and purchases some skinny jeans, v-neck sweater, adorbs scarf, and enough accessories to overwhelm Liz Taylor. Basic, right? And all for under $40. Lord knows she does not have the money to be buying another new outfit but this was somewhat of a fashion emergency.

As Dulilah drives home, she comes to the most tasking decision of the day. Go home and get ready or hurry to the gym to workout. She had already been to a spin class that morning but those skinny jeans were feeling really skinny. Gym for sure.

See what you don't know about Dulilah is that she is about 5'7" and weighs in at about 140 pounds. She has a banging body. She, however, does not know she has a great body. She has spent most of her life in a battle of the body. She has managed to convince herself that she is morbidly obese and obsesses over every calorie, carb and curve. Her goal weight remains at "Less than I am right now."

Dulilah runs in the kitchen and grabs a quick diet coke to pound while she is getting ready. She needs all the energy she can to bust out a fierce workout. She then proceeds to put on an outfit far too matchy and cute for the gym and a full face of makeup. She grabs her purse and makes a run for the front door. Shit. She forgot something. She runs upstairs and gives herself a squirt of perfume. Ready now.

The gym: an absolutely god awful nightmare for Dulilah. Aside from the fact that she manages to run into 17 people she knows while she is there, they all manage to look thinner than her and have whiter teeth than her. She has somehow managed to turn this angst into motivation to run harder and cycle faster. Envy is a powerful motivator; possibly the most powerful. *And most unhealthy, mind you.* She runs into Lynn. They give each other a big ass-out hug and carry on for about 15 minutes of shallow and mind numbing conversation before parting ways to their respective machines. "Bye girl! Love you Lynn! Call me!" Dulilah hated Lynn.

After a good 45 minutes of treadmill and elliptical, Dulilah realizes she has to go! She has a date with her boyfriend tonight and she only has 3 hours to get ready and be at his doorstep. The process of getting ready takes about 1 hour and 15 minutes, but it is always best to add a cushion of an hour to make sure everything is perfect from head to freshly painted toes.

After shitting, showering, shaving, plucking, applying, dressing, and teasing, Dulilah is ready. And for what you ask? Is she heading out to a Broadway play? Is it some sort of masquerade ball she is attending with the Mayor of Ocean Beach? A fashion show for the thrifty shopper? No, no, no. It is something far more special and romantic than that. It is Friday date night and she is going to her boyfriend's apartment…to watch a movie.

Womp, womp.

He said to be over around 6, so at 5:45, she leaves her house and sits in her car. She waits a couple minutes, because she can't be at his house at exactly 6. That might look weird and desperate. Around 5:49pm, she heads over. She jams out to Natasha Beddingfield, Taylor Swift and other delusional love songs. She sometimes feels like the songs are written for her. They are nothing like her situation, but she has somehow tricked herself into thinking that the lyrics were about a couple just like her and Sid.

Meet Sid. Sid is Dulilah's boyfriend. Sid was *that* guy; the arrogant, self-absorbed, ill-mannered dude that nobody seemed to like but managed to have an entourage of dudes. He wore embroidered jeans. Sometimes, on special occasions, he wore his bedazzled embroidered jeans. And try not to be overpowered by the scent of his hair product. Sid: Douche bag. He was exactly her type.

So Sid opens the door and it is like a scene from a movie. She sees a prince swinging his hair back and forth and shining armor from toes to glorious head. Everyone else sees an ogre. Nonetheless, she excitedly enters the house for the extravagant plans he has made. He had told her he would plan something special and she was practically sweating with anticipation over the grand ordeal he had in store. She hadn't mentioned but it was their two year anniversary tomorrow. Kind of a big deal. He obviously was going to surprise her with something. As she enters into his bachelor pad, he explains that he was starving but hadn't made any food plans. She quickly offers to cook up something. Shucks. He doesn't have enough ingredients to make a sandwich. Shit, he doesn't even have the ingredients to make toast. She offers to go to the store and buy some dinner and make a nice meal for the two of them. He confesses he would rather order pizza. Dulilah doesn't like pizza and never has liked pizza. Sid is well aware of this but doesn't seem to pay any attention to that minor detail. Forty five minutes later the four course meal arrives. He pays for the pizza, wings, salad and bread sticks. What a guy. As they eat, she makes sure she only eats 2 pieces of pizza, carefully picking off the pepperoni and cheese. Part of her is genuinely afraid of being fat while the other part of her wants to make sure that Sid knows that she is watching her caloric intake.

After dinner, they sit quietly on the couch watching some sort of sports recap show. She is quietly hoping he might mention something about a movie to watch, but is careful not to disrupt the program he is enjoying. Dulilah even manages to ask a few questions about the sport and seem somewhat interested. After about an hour, he hands her the remote and announces he needs to change his shirt. Oh, okay. Dulilah sits on the couch alone and flips through the channels. She was trying to find something that would be enjoyable for both of them, but it seemed virtually impossible, seeing as how their interests were on polar ends of the spectrum. After about 15 minutes of flipping through reality TV and murder mystery stories, she realizes his shirt changing task was taking just a bit too long. She calls his name and he opens the door and he comes bursting out of his room telling her to relax. He is wearing the exact same shirt he went in the room with 15 minutes ago. She is puzzled, but she says nothing. Maybe he has two bedazzled v-neck t-shirts. He instantly complains about the shit she has on TV. He grabs the remote and starts flipping, one leg up on the couch and one arm over the head, leaving no room for any affectionate movement or physical contact.

Feeling a bit defeated and not wanting him to sense it, she excuses herself to the bathroom. She needed to check her face and her quickly souring attitude. She leans into the mirror to apply a layer of gloss and makes sure the part in her hair was the way she arranged it when she left her house. She hears her phone make the text message alert. It was probably her un-approving sister nagging at her. She reaches inside her purse and realizes there is no text. Hallucinations. About 60 seconds later, the noise rings again, as iPhone notifications do when a text is received and unopened. Hum. Nothing. Although with a slight delay, she eventually realizes the noise is not her phone. She starts glancing around the room trying to determine the origination of the noise. Bingo. It is Sid's phone. There it is, laying face up on his bed, all lit up with a new notification on the screen.

And here we have the age old debate of whether it is acceptable to pick up the phone and read the text or leave it alone. Sure we should trust our significant other and not have the burden of monitoring their life, but in the battle of common sense and insecurity, insecurity will always win. Without an ounce of hesitation, Dulilah picked up the phone and went to read the text. Perhaps it was her insecurity, perhaps it was her common sense, or perhaps it was her obsession with texting that made it an uncontrollable force of nature to reach for that phone. Damn. Password protected.

Being that Sid wasn't a particularly intelligent creature and Dulilah was smart as a whip and motivated by the intense burn of growing curiosity, it only took two guesses to figure out the password. 2688. The last four numbers of his cell phone number. Brilliant. She was almost shocked she had never scrolled through his phone before. He always seemed to have it in his pocket. She was immediately disappointed to discover the wallpaper on his phone was some racecar and not a picture of her. As the phone unlocked, she glances at the door to make sure Sid didn't walk in on her invading his privacy. The shame was beginning to set in, so she moved quickly before it overtook her conscious and ruined her plan. **New text from Nicole.** Who is Nicole? The text reads "When is she leaving?" Instant nausea. Dulilah already knew. Dulilah begins to feel dizzy and feels her body move from a quiet shake to a tremble. She tried to swallow but her throat felt like it was closing. She wanted to move her thumb to scroll down the screen and see what preceded this question, but her hands were shaking so bad that she couldn't manage to move. As if any of this mattered at all. She already knew what happened before that question. It was her worst nightmare that she had lived in her head a thousand times. It was the situation she had tried so desperately to avoid happening that she practically willed it to happen to her.

Her thumb shakes across the screen and the conversation between Sid and Nicole is revealed.

Nicole: Miss you. Off work at 10. Hang?
Sid: For sure. Text me when you're off. D is coming over so DL.
Nicole: Boo. Tell her you're tired. LOL.
Sid: I know. Have fun at work.
Nicole: When is she leaving?

Dulilah went from having the shakes to being absolutely frozen still. It had happened. Her ugliest and most intense fear had come to life. She couldn't move. She couldn't think. She went numb. She sat down and stared into the dark tunnel of heart break. Have you ever seen glass shatter? The way it breaks into a million tiny little pieces in such a beautiful way. Her heart combusted inside her chest and she felt the tiny little pieces settle into the bottom of her stomach. She looked at the ground hoping to find her soul had leaked out of the bottom of her boot and she could salvage what was left into a reusable bottle.

"Dulilah!" Sid is yelling from the television room.

"Fuck. Snap out of it. Fuck. What do I do?" Dulilah couldn't seem to get a hold of the thoughts in her head long enough to make a rational decision about what to do next. She glances at the time on Sid's phone. It was 9:18. She tries to get a hold of herself. She decides she can't bear confronting him and decides to pretend she did not see the message. She gives him the benefit of the doubt. If he lets her stay past 10, it will mean the text was nothing and Nicole is nobody and the night can go on perfect as it was supposed to be. It will be like that text message alert was never even heard and no conversation was ever read. Done.

Composed, Dulilah walks out to the television room and is on what seems to be a mission to win Sid. She sits on his lap and asks what he wants to do now. She starts to run her fingers through his hair. He has always loved that. After a good 8 seconds, he pulls his eyes away from the television and look at her with a sideways glance. And then it happens. He releases the most bullshit, contrived version of a yawn and declares that he is tired. He explains he is tired from working all day and he thinks he wants to make it an early night.

The glass shatters again.

This time she cannot hide the pain. Her bottom lip begins to uncontrollably quiver, as though she finally allowed the emotions to rush out of her body all at once. She buries her hands in her face and releases at least three minutes of hysterical ugly cry and allows the makeup she worked so hard to apply to sadly melt off of her face. She loses all care about her appearance and moves into a state of honest desperation. Sid goes from shock, to annoyance, to anger at the outburst Dulilah is displaying. He asks repeatedly what she is freaking out about and expresses how dumb she is for being mad that he wants to sleep. She finally pulls her face out of her hands and through all the tears and snot and melted mascara manages one lonely and painful word. "Nicole."

He quickly changes...everything. His voice. His demeanor. His tone. His facial muscles. He flies into a panic that his plan has been uncovered. He stands up and starts jumping from one thought to another, but Dulilah is deaf. She is unreachable. Nothing he says will relieve the pain her body is feeling. Like a living zombie, she stands up, grabs her purse and walks out the front door. Sid follows her to the door warning her of all the terrible things that will happen if she walks out that door. He slams the door and she starts her car.

The car ride home was deafening silence; from what she can remember. Dulilah stared ahead into the distance like a robot. Tears were streaming down her face but there was no sound or movement accompanying the flow. There was no music, no noise, and no cars around her. She simply drove the 12 minute drive home staring hundreds of miles into the distance.

An unhealthy soul is easily broken.

As she pulls into the circular drive of her house, she turns off her car and stares at the center of the steering wheel. It is as though her brain has turned off to shield her from the pain of what she is experiencing. It must be some sort of survival mechanism for the weak of heart and those who are void of self worth. She leaves everything in her car and walks straight to her bedroom. She removes her shoes and that is all she has the energy to do. She lies down and the comfort of her pillow allows her to release a deep and heavy cry. She is sure to be quiet so nobody in the house will hear her pain. Pain at its worst is deserving of a certain level of privacy. The tears flow out so violently and relentlessly it is though they have been stored in her body for years.

Unable to quiet her mind and knowing the torture of the night that was about to take place, Dulilah quietly crept downstairs to find relief. Her mom had a prescription for anxiety medication and it seemed it was the only thing that could get her through the night. She rummaged through the dark cabinet and found the orange bottle. Her hand shook as she grabbed two oval shaped emotional pain relievers and swallowed them dry.

She returns to her room and lays her head on her wet pillow. She flips it over and a new river flows from her eyes. Twenty minutes later, she escapes to her dreams.

Saturday, 10:30am

Dulilah opens her eyes and is surprised at how bright the sun is shining in her room. It is the first time in weeks that she is awake after the sun. She gives a long stretch and hears her joints crack. She takes a moment and enjoys the freedom she feels at that very moment. She sits up and looks down at her nighttime attire and laughs aloud at herself for falling asleep in the full ensemble from the night before. Then she laughs at the sight of her jeans with their perfect little mascara polka dots on them. She could have sworn that mascara was waterproof. She reaches for her phone and sees 17 missed calls. Eleven are from Sid, four are from Savvy and two are from her sister. Geez. Can a girl sleep in on a Saturday? She flips her blankets off of her and grabs a bottle of water off her dresser and pounds the entire thing in 30 seconds flat. Those 16 ounces replenished all the tears she had cried from the previous night and flushed her soul all at once. She enters the kitchen with a raging appetite and decides that she wants spaghetti. Sure, spaghetti isn't a breakfast food, but it sounded so delicious at that very moment. Technically it was almost lunchtime. So she boiled some water, cooked up some meat and made herself a heaping plate of pasta. And what better to wash it down than a glass of whole milk? It must've been the carbs because after that Dulilah had a surge of energy. It was already well after 11 and she had missed all the classes at the gym. Glancing outside, she sees the weather is a typical beautiful San Diego sunny day and decides she is going to take a towel down to the beach and do her yoga on the beach. She hadn't been to the beach in forever, which is particularly sad since she lives less than 20 minutes away and had always loved the beach. She runs upstairs, throws on some clothes, grabs a towel and heads west.

As she drives down the road, she stops at the stop light right in front of Sid's apartment complex. She looks over to her left and sees Sid's house. She stares that direction for a bit and then brings her eyes back to the road. She looks down at her radio and turns it up as the light turns green. She drives on and experiences a moment. She didn't know what that moment was or where it came from, but she tilted her head to the right and kind of pursed her lips. She had this brief moment where she felt sorry for Sid. When she extracted herself from the situation, she realized he wasn't capable of loving. He had a very tumultuous childhood and had such poor role models in the field of love that Dulilah felt a bit of compassion. This man might never know true love and might even sabotage any chance that he has of attaining it. The irony.

As she pulls up to the beach, she finds parking right up front. Score! She gets out and stares at the water for a while. Dulilah had always been a skeptic of all things religion but she did always say that if there were a heaven it would be this stretch of beach. She marches down the stairs and finds a perfect spot just yards away from the water. And just as though she had an instructor on front of her, she went through her entire 50 minute yoga routine. At the end of her session, she sits down, crosses her legs and begins the closing meditation with the gentle sounds of the ocean waves rolling in the background. Just as she was dancing through the peaceful thoughts in her head, she hears the jingle jangle of a dog collar coming closer and closer. She opens her eyes to find a giant dog David Hasselhoff-ing down the beach. It stops right in front of Dulilah. The dog comes over in all his slobbery glory and lays down right on her towel. Realizing this big canine is harmless; she gives him a nice little wrestle and looks around the beach for a potential owner. From behind her she hears a man's voice yelling for the pup. She turns around and it's her friend JP from high school. My God, it had been years since she had seen JP.

"Hey JP! Long time, no see stranger! Is this your hairy friend?"

"Yeah, this is my baby boy. Ralph."

"Well if you are going to name your goofy dog after a human I suppose his name should be Ralph."

He squatted down and they chatted for a little more than ten minutes. He explained he worked for the fire department and they often did their workouts on the beach. Dulilah explained she usually didn't work out on the beach but had decided she would from now on. He told her how much he loved the beach and how he was sure that God had created the ocean to assure us that there was a heaven. She marinated in that thought for a few seconds and agreed with a smile. He carried on with Ralph and his jog.

Dulilah enjoyed another 10 minutes of sun before she rolled up her towel and made her way back to her car. It was only 1:00pm and she had the entire day ahead of her. She grabs for her phone to call her friend Savvy and sees she has six missed calls from Sid. Call number seven was about to happen.

At that moment, Dulilah had a heavy decision to make. Should she answer the phone? What does she say? What is there to say? She had already decided. Did she need to include him in the decision?

"Hello?"

"Why the fuck aren't you answering your phone?" Sid is yelling and Dulilah is as calm as the ocean she sees in front of her. There is an immense peace that comes from deciding. Deciding you are worth more. Deciding you want more. Deciding what you deserve. She calmly replied to his hysteria.

"I am sorry if I worried you. I was at the beach. Did you need to talk about something? Because I want to assure you that I do not need any explanations and I understand where your heart is. I wish you all the best and I don't want you to feel any guilt for what happened with us yesterday or the past couple years."

The silence on the other end went on for such a long period of time that Dulilah had to glance at her phone to make sure the call was still connected.

"Sid?"

She heard labored breathing and what sounded like a man crying. She had never seen or heard Sid cry so she was sure that was not the source of the sound. Then the hysterics and pleading began.

"Dulilah. I am so sorry. I have never been so sorry about anything in my life. I swear to God I will never ever do anything wrong ever again. This bitch just kept calling me and I couldn't cut her off because I am too nice. I swear this will never happen again. Please God. I understand now. Please come over and we can have a perfect day together. We can go do that hike you have always wanted to do. Please. Please. God, don't freak out. We are gonna be fine. I will make it okay."

This was the emotion that Dulilah had wanted from Sid for so long. She had prayed that one day he would want her the way she wanted him. He had finally shown up and she had already left the building.

"Sid. I am so glad that you apologized. I can hear in your voice that you mean it. I also know that whatever we had is broken and I don't want to put it back together. I hope you understand. I also hope you understand when I tell you I don't want to speak with you for a very long time. Possibly never again. I wish you and your family the very best and I can walk away right now knowing that I gave all of myself to a person and I can take all of that person back. I am going to hang up now and I want this to be the last time we discuss any of this. Goodbye."

She hung up and exhaled. It was like the last breath of a dying relationship. Flat line. The phone rang. She declined and drove down coast highway. She placed her phone on silent and face down on her center console. She decided she was going to go for a hike. She had always wanted to do this epic hike that everyone talks about in La Jolla. She had begged Sid to take her there for the past two years because it looked like suck a romantic place to go. She had always seen people posting photos of the hike and kissing at the top. Today was a perfect day to conquer that hike.

She spent the next three hours climbing Mount La Jolla. The view at the top was even more beautiful than the pictures on Facebook. She had decided that if heaven wasn't the beach she was at this morning, it was the top of this mountain. She got to the top and took a picture of herself at the top blowing a kiss to the camera. She posted it on Facebook with the caption "Kisses from the top of the world." She made her descent back to the parking lot and to her car. As she unlocked her car, she looked at her reflection in the car window. She was wearing dirty pajamas that she decided could double as gym clothes and her makeup was the melted residual of the night before. She was a mess. She had never felt more beautiful in all her life.

On her way home, she drove through her favorite fast food place. She hadn't eaten there in years and had promised she would never indulge in that shit again. She seemed to forget about all that when she ordered the largest combo they had and enjoyed every last bite on the drive home. She had the music blasting. She had no idea who the artist was or what the song was, but it was perfect.

When she arrived back home it was dark and her parents were home. She walked in and they gave her a once over and asked "Are you okay?" Their eyes were filled with sympathy as if they knew the last 24 hours had been hell. "I am good but I am exhausted. I am going to go shower and call it a night." They didn't know how to respond. They were all prepared for her to have an emotional meltdown. Her stability was a shock.

In the shower she went. She washed away the leftover makeup, the sweat from the workouts, and all of the emotions from the night before. She brushed her teeth and took a deep breath through her minty mouth. She put on her cozy pajamas and lay down in her bed. Within minutes she was sound asleep.

If you were to go downstairs and into the cabinet, you would find an orange bottle with white oval shaped pills. In that bottle would be the pills that Dulilah had taken the night before. She had thought they were her emotional pain relievers. As it turns out, she did not take her mother's Xanax as she had intended. She had taken 5,000mg of Confidence.

Eat Like A Boss Bitch.

If you are what you eat, I recommend you have yourself a large bowl of classy bitch every morning with some sugar on top. And while you are at it, do an extra hour of classy bitchercising because Lord knows you want to look good and feel even better. In order to keep your classy bitch machine running at its highest and best capacity, you are going to have to acknowledge that you can't be putting cheap oil down the chute and you can't be sending it to the sleezeball mechanic down the street. You are going to have to cut the habits you had when you were young and perhaps read a box or two. Your body is a Tesla, not a Honda.

DISCLAIMER: I am not about to tell you what diet regimen you should follow or give you a daily chart of what to shove into your pie hole. I do not know the magic secret formula to losing cellulite and I have no idea what exercise you should do to tone your knee caps. I am, however, going to give you a swift kick in the mental gut. After all, that is what it took for me to snap out of my hypoglycemic haze.

It was the summer of 2010. We had just bought our first house and had decided we would need to cut some expenses. Yay. Being that I was unwilling to give up my hairdresser and we agreed electricity would be a necessity, we decided one sacrifice we would make would be cable. I consoled myself by assuring my inner teenager that we would watch 'The Real World' at my parents' house and that I could stream 'Housewives' on the internet. My husband helped to soothe my worst fears by purchasing a membership to Netflix. This way we could still watch movies and the kids could still watch educational and informative programs such as Fraggle Rock and Dora the Explorer. All would be fine in the world.

As Netflix and I became good friends and eventually sisters, I became addicted to some of the series it offered. I spent an entire week watching every episode from every season of 'House' ever made. I could not pull my ass off the couch. I think I thought I was learning or participating in some sort of educational activity.

After each show, I was able to convince myself I had the ailment he discovered during that episode. I am still nervous about my fingernails turning blue due to an increase in copper thanks to Dr. House and his medical mysteries. 'House' was the least of my worries. I was about to travel down a path of horrific educational moments in the form of…dun, dun, dun…documentaries.

Nobody warns you of the perils of documentaries. The fact you are watching something so intense and it actually bears some truth takes all the fun and innocence out of it all. The closest thing I had ever watched to a documentary was Titanic and that movie fucked me up. It all started with a harmless documentary about Fast Food. I had already watched the film during a class I had taken in college but I am pretty sure at the time I watched it I weighed 120 pounds and wore size zero Abercrombie jeans. Suddenly my post-baby 160 pound body was paying attention to the little factoids they were sharing about calories and fat consumption. Okay, fine. You're right. I decided it was time to cut fast food out of my diet. It wasn't too much of a change since we rarely ate at fast food restaurants and had agreed eating out would be one of the costs we would cut. Plus I was getting tired of getting diarrhea every time I did decide to indulge in a drive-thru meal. Sounds pretty basic, right? Eliminate fast food and carry on.

I wish. Netflix took it a step further and decided to ruin my life a little more. It did this clever little thing called "Recommended for You." It decided that because I watched a documentary about the evils of fast food, I might also like this documentary about criminal corn. So I went ahead and trusted my beloved sister and I watched the documentary about corn. Son of a bitch. This film decided to share all sorts of horrifying and devastating facts about the food I consume everyday and pretty much ruin anything I planned on enjoying in my cupboard. All of a sudden I had all of this knowledge that I had previously preferred to blissfully ignore. Unfortunately, I could no longer do that. After about SEVEN documentaries that Netflix decided to "recommend" to me, I was afraid to eat anything and everything. I had turned my back on brands I had been loyal to my entire life. I started trashing foods in my cabinet and pretty much emptied all but the ice in my freezer;

an awesomely tragic move in a time of money saving and coupon clipping. My usual trips to the grocery store went from one hour to over three hours as I obsessively read every single ingredient and percentage on the packaging. While I am proud that I was becoming a healthier and more knowledgeable consumer, I was legitimately afraid of food. I couldn't eat a meal without worrying about the origin, the factory it came from and its hygienic guidelines, the sodium levels, the transportation method and whether it had GMO's. It was a beautiful time of awakening and metamorphosis in my life.

You see, diet is NOT about trend. It is not about the fastest way to lose a pound and it is not about the easiest way to achieve your goal weight. I am a firm believer that every human body has its own DNA and genetic makeup that requires a diet plan as individual as the fingerprint which it is attached. The Paleo diet might work great for the lumberjack down the street but not for the hippie at the elementary school. The blood type diet might work great for the engineer and terribly for the town vampire. The reason that diets start riots is because they are impulsive, temporary and a modern day form of torture. I can bet that 90% of classy bitches reading this have successfully lost weight through the latest diet fad, and successfully gained it back by acting like a normally functioning human.

The diet I recommend, endorse and stamp with my seal of classy bitch approval is EDUCATION. If you learn about the food you are eating, you are going to eat the best food that nature can provide. Ignorance is not bliss, it is obesity. It is high blood pressure and shitty skin and everything that a classy bitch is not. Once you start to accumulate knowledge about the foods you are consuming, an amazing thing happens. You start to eat healthy without even so much as a struggle. Food begins to make sense and blood begins to flow. What I once experienced as FEAR towards food has been translated into an understanding of my body and the food that enters my body palace. Once I started eating what my body enjoyed, I started feeling more energetic. And once I started feeling more energetic, I craved physical activity. Without even making a conscious effort, I started losing weight. I did not have a goal weight in mind and I did not aspire to look like that bitch Giselle when wearing a bikini. I simply wanted to feel and look as fierce as I possibly could. I came to the realization that you don't know how shitty you feel until you start feeling good.

After reading some books, watching some videos, watching "recommended" documentaries, and experimenting with my personal diet, I made some big decisions about my lifestyle. For one, I decided I didn't want to eat meat anymore. While this was a decision that worked out fabulously for me and my thighs, I would never impose it on my husband or kids. I don't even endorse vegetarianism. I endorse making informed decisions. It is really easy for me to stay committed to my decision to abstain from meat because I have done the footwork. I have images implanted into my brain and statistics stamped into my subconscious that motivate me every day to stay away from meat. For example, anytime I see a hot dog, I don't think, "My damn diet forbids me from eating anything remotely tasty." Instead, I go back to all the fucked up documentaries I watched and the videos that haunt me and any urge, impulse or craving to eat that shit sausage disappears.

Unfortunately, thanks to the likes of Facebook, Twitter, YouTube, and the world wide wizeb, you can no longer plead ignorance when it comes to your food. All the information you need to become an educated eater is a click away. Ten years ago it was understandable when a mother didn't know the food on her kid's plate was made of cardboard and horse hair. It was the beginning of the processed food revolution. Plus we didn't have social media so bad news traveled much slower. Nowadays, you can research every aspect of your lunch from last Tuesday in 45 minutes. With all of the media hysteria about GMO's, processed foods, food contamination, obesity and high blood pressure, you have got to be a god damn fool to not question every molecule in your meal. What you eat could be killing you and you don't even know it! It is possible I am being a bit dramatic but my point is simply that you need to do your research. When I conducted my research, my whole world changed. If you do your research and you are still perfectly okay with eating fast food, then high fucking five. Research is all I am asking you to do. Change is optional.

Keep in mind that you are a responsible and classy bitch and I recommend you spend three beers or a half bottle of wine being a smarty pants. Go online and start Googling and typing and reading and gathering as much information as you can about food. It is entirely possible you will decide you are doing a splendid job at your current diet and no changes are necessary. It is more likely that you will realize that in order to honor your worldly duty of being the classiest bitch you can possibly be, a few changes are in order. Change is only possible when backed by passion and motivation. Passion and motivation can be as easy to attain as a subscription to Netflix. You got this.

By the way, you are allowed to drink those three beers or half bottle of wine. As long as you are educated about the implications it will have on your body and sleep patterns, then have at it. In this case, you are not ignorant; you are just in the mood to party. An educated drunk is much more acceptable than an ignorant drunk. And to that, I say bottoms up!

Green Straw University

I am not sure if picking a college major at the age of 17 should be legal in the United States. I am pretty sure I could have opened my California State University Welcome packet, closed my eyes and pointed at a major and it would have been equally as effective as the major I chose. How is one to commit to what they want to do for the next 38 years of their life? How was I, at the ripe age of 17, supposed to responsibly invest tens of thousands of dollars in a topic when I hadn't even had a menstrual cycle for two years? The whole ordeal is incredibly risky and irresponsible. If I had been passionate about cutting hair or putting out house fires then that would have been a whole other story. I would have enrolled in a specialty school and saved my parents a shit ton of money.

Hindsight is always 20/20. That sonova bitch must have had Lasik. Needless to say I am a 30 year old with 75% of a degree which is about as useful as tits on a bull. The good news is that I am readily equipped with advice for my kids when it comes time to enroll in a school. Don't bother going until you know where you're *going*. I close my eyes and envision this conversation in my head. I have my hands on my hips and I am advising my boys in a very hillbilly accent and at the end I pucker my lips. I can't wait to deliver those wise words. I cannot wait to save tens of thousands of dollars on their responsible education choices.

While I did not attain my degree from California State University, I did manage to get several degrees from another well-known university; Green Straw University. Green Straw University is not an academic institute but a well-known coffee shop whose name I cannot legally reveal. *Hint: overpriced designer coffee with a green straw.* That is right. For ten whole years I was a legal drug dealer on the streets of suburbia. My drug of choice was caffeine and I learned more behind that counter than I ever would have learned in a lecture hall. I earned a PhD in Psychology, Sociology, and Politics, all while wearing a green apron and a shit-eating grin. I don't know what it is about a coffee shop but it reveals more about human behavior than most of the text books I read in my sociology classes at Cal State San Marcos. There were times I felt like the mayor of my town because I served the citizens their java. And there were times I felt like a diary because I held some of the town's worst secrets.

There is something about a coffee shop that makes people feel right at home. I have decided it is America's favorite place to take a shit and Baristas are their favorite person to share their life story. I think it is because we are trained to be obnoxiously nice and they develop this belief that we are genuinely interested. It is also because I am making them their next fix. It makes it a comfortable environment for emotional hand holding and verbal vomit.

The strangest thing about a coffee shop is that it makes people feel safe enough to have an affair; an extramarital affair. I wonder if pizza places get jealous that adulterers don't choose their lobby. In my decade at Green Straw Cafe, I can remember witnessing four serious affairs. I am suspicious of at least a dozen more. I would love to share all twelve of these stories but there was one in particular that really changed my view of affairs and humanity.

It was the first affair I ever witnessed and it was after two years of working at this one store. I was the ripe and naïve age of 19. I stumbled upon the man whore and his mistress while sitting on the patio outside the store on my lunch break. I had this awesome trick where I would put headphones on even if I wasn't listening to music. I did this so customers wouldn't come and talk to me on my break. While I loved hearing about their first world problems, I needed those ten minute breaks to recharge my batteries. Headphones are the universal sign that you are socially unavailable. On this particular evening, my anti-social antics delivered the most riveting conversation behind me. I realize now that they thought I couldn't hear them and therefore felt safe to have their dirty and dark conversation. These fucking idiots didn't realize I could hear every whisper and giggle from my seat two feet behind them. Looking back now, I didn't even have to listen to them to know they were having an affair. Only one of them had a wedding band, they were abnormally affectionate, and they both looked so paranoid you would think they were about to engage in a high profile Columbian drug deal.

Their conversation started off super friendly about his business and she went on about her job that she hated. She started saying things like, "I can't wait until we can be together and I don't have to work anymore." They spoke in some sort of code about certain "roommates" and "coworkers." As if they had broken the ice and were ready for the real reason they were sitting there, the conversation started getting juicy. They leaned in closer and they started talking about how his WIFE almost caught him the other night. At that point I was worried they might have heard the light bulb go off in my head. HOLY SHIT! They *are* having an affair. He was talking about how after he left her place the other night, he went home and he knew he smelled like sex. He became very concerned that his wife might want to be intimate when he returned home and he knew that his junk still reeked of that funky "condom smell." The mistress listening on the other side of the table looked like she was excited by the anticipation of the story and had this giddy laugh. At one point I heard her clapping her hands. I wanted to turn around and clap her across the face, then spit on her, and then give her a hug. The poor thing thought she was special. She probably had more psychological baggage than anybody would ever know and this ordeal would only end in more baggage and a serious need for counseling.

Well as his story unfolds, he comes home and immediately gets in the shower and the wife becomes suspicious because it is out of character. The wife then asks to see his phone and proceeded to call the most recent numbers. He proudly boasts that he erased all their communications and so she only called a few of his clients. They both laugh and talk about their "luck." At this point I realized my ten minute break was up and I needed to return back to work but I was terrified to stand up. I didn't want to draw attention to the fact that their affair had a captive audience. As soon as they left, I returned back from my break and tried my best to digest what the fuck just happened outside. I am well aware that it is not my responsibility to police the love lives of the whores in my community but it also didn't feel right to walk back to work and continue grinding beans. I wish there was some sort of anonymous hotline to report this shit. My conscious felt heavy and I didn't even do anything.

Well as it turns out, this man whore was a regular at my store. I had never noticed him before because I had never had any interaction with him worth remembering. So you can imagine my surprise when I realized this douche bag came in once and sometimes twice a day. He purchased the same drink every time; a grande medium roast with room for cream. Each time he came in I felt my stomach do a back flip over my kidney and a severe wind of nausea from the mere sight of his filth. Sometimes I had planned to say something and other times I just had my own version of revenge and served him with decaf coffee. He was actually a relatively nice guy and he would sometimes try and get chummy with me. I would give him my best passive aggressive bitch reply. He had no clue that I knew his dirty little secret. Until one Sunday morning…

It was busy as hell and I was working the coffee bar. I glance up from steaming milk for a moment and in walks man whore with his wife…his VERY PREGNANT wife. My jaw hit the countertop and I nearly knocked over everything within an arm's reach. At that moment, and for reasons I can't understand, I felt a huge burden of guilt. It was like I had some duty as a responsible woman and citizen of humanity to tell this child-bearer about the man standing to her right. I couldn't even make eye contact as they walked in holding hands. The worst part is they both looked happy. Not a sign of misery or despondency. They order their drinks, his usual medium roast and a decaf mocha for the wife. As they stood there and waited for me to finish making the espresso beverage, I look up and cannot prevent the mild verbal vomit that is about to spew out of my mouth.

"Hey there Bill. Welcome back! It feels like you were just here. Oh that's right…You *were* just here last night! You can't get enough of our coffee can you?! Where is your friend?" And then I connect with his eyes for about 15 seconds and I don't break eye contact. If looks could kill, this man would have hit the floor face first, aorta spurting blood and his body flailing on the tile like a fish out of water. It was at that moment that Bill realized that I was aware of his dirty little secret. He nervously played with the cardboard sleeve on his coffee cup and gave me a nod and a smile. His wife simply stood there, in all her innocence, and gave me a cute little smile and an adorable pregnant shrug. All that I wanted to say in that moment fermented in my cerebrum and never exited through my lips. How badly I wanted to sit her down and do her the favor of informing her, while simultaneously ruining her life. But I knew it was not my place to change the course of their universe. The only thing I could do was make sure this skeezebag didn't feel safe with his secret around me. In the coming weeks after this visit, he still came in every morning. He tried his very hardest to befriend me and kiss my ass. I treated him like a cold sore on the ass of a pig. He never came in again with his mistress. And although I don't know for sure what happened with the triangle, I can make a safe guess.

I can guess that he eventually left his mistress in the dust while she crumbled into a million insecure pieces. The mistress was planning on a happily ever after and instead was used like a tissue. His wife birthed their baby and he continued loving her with a hint of guilt, but a slight measure of pleasure that he had gotten away with it. Bill probably cheated again with another fragile victim. He was bored with his wife and had the attention span of a goldfish. His wife would never acknowledge the distance between them because their life was comfortable and avoiding pain is much easier than facing it.

As it turns out, I didn't have to live my life wondering what happened to Bill and his pregnant wife. Years later, I was going through a photo album at a "friends" house and would you know it? I see man-whore-Bill in one of their photos, smiling like shit-eating scum. I practically yelled at my friend while demanding to know how she knew Bill. Apparently he was a good friend of their family. It's a small world after all. She told me about their adorable little toddler and how the company he owned was doing really well. I digested the update and then it happened. I spilled absolutely everything I knew about Bill and his dirty little secret. I told my friend about the conversation I heard on the patio, about the pregnant wife on that Sunday morning, and about the weird guilt I had felt for being witness to this emotional crime. It was as though I finally felt safe telling someone since enough time had passed. It also felt like I was somehow passing the buck of responsibility onto my friend. If she wanted to say something, go right ahead. I also had some underlying intention of tainting his reputation and the obnoxiously false perception people had of him.

In a completely un-shocking turn of events, she never said a word. Apparently it is too large of a burden to crumble someone's universe. Perhaps this is why so many people get away with affairs. Bystanders are not trying to protect the whore committing adultery; they are trying to protect the vulnerable spouse. Irony.

This little incident taught me a lot about myself and human behavior. It was the first time I was a third wheel in an affair. And it was the last time I would have my headphones on without music. In the coming years, I would witness three more affairs of this magnitude and from such a close proximity. Each of these four affairs was exactly the same. They bared the same features, the same characteristics, and the same outcome. The man never left his wife for the mistress. The mistress was always younger and more vulnerable. The marriage was always seemingly happy. They always picked a coffee shop as their cheating grounds.

Green Straw Cafe was like one big social experiment. After ten years of watching people come in and out the doors of my store, I had picked up on human behavior patterns and stereotypes like a modern day fucking Freud. Within seconds of someone placing their beverage order, I had their number. I knew their type. While I admit that my model is far from perfect, it is accurate enough that I was able to create a formula and pass it on to you lucky bastards as a tool for you in your further social interactions.

If you are ever in a situation where you need to assess the character of someone, say a first date, job interview, new neighbor assessment, I am offering you this formula as a handy reference.

"Hello *Potential Future Spouse and Breeding Partner*, my name is Jennie. **What drink do you order at Green Straw Cafe?"**

Boom. Right there. That is it. The answer to this question holds more of a character indicator than the type of car they drive, the job they have, and their relationship with their mother. Allow me to explain.

First. As a general rule, the more syllables in a person's drink order, the bigger the ass-hat. Like on a scale of 1-30 syllables, the lower the number the more likeable the person. If someone tells you that they order a triple grande, sugar free cinnamon dulce, nonfat, no foam, one sugar, extra hot latte, that means they order a 22 syllable drink and they are pretty high on the scale. Immediate red flag! This person is as high maintenance as they come. If they were a car, they would be a 1969 Porsche and it would be bright yellow. This could be fun, but be warned that they are probably high maintenance in every arena of their life and are more prone to make a scene at the grocery store because the checker won't accept their expired coupon. You know the type. It might be your type. Just be prepared. Similarly, if someone orders a tall coffee, they're sitting solid at three syllables. Good people. Salt of the earth people.

To make the process easier, I have made some generalizations for you. You might find that you fall comfortably into one of these categories and might want to either laugh or cuss me out. Both are completely acceptable. Either way, I'm right.

Time out. Did you just realize your drink is 42 syllables? It's all good. Take this time to reevaluate your life. Your life will be just fine without the extra 15 degrees in your beverage. Having a longer coffee drink order might make you feel important but I assure you there is so much more to life. Take it easy cowboy.

THE BLACK COFFEE
The Black Coffee keeps it simple. They don't have time for bullshit and fluff. They are probably annoyed at the fact that they even buy coffee from the Green Straw Cafe but it is the strongest

coffee they can find and they know it will taste the same every time. They used to buy coffee from the gas station but decided to take it up a notch when the coffee at the gas station required chewing. Black Coffee is a very habitual person and has been doing the same routines and activities for the past 50% of their life. They have no intentions of changing things up and they can't believe the shit that these yuppy people do to their coffee. The Black Coffee still wonders what the fuck a macchiato means. They believe technology is the downfall of society and they remember the good old days when people read the newspaper and gas was fifty nine cents. If you call the black coffee on their cell phone, they will have to unfold the phone to answer it. They are a pretty down to earth person and they find happiness in simplicity. The Black Coffee makes for a great mate but don't expect flowers and chocolates. Instead, expect loyalty and consistency. Expect the fights to be short because the Black Coffee doesn't play games and straight shoots ya right between the eyes. Black Coffee probably has an evening beverage routine as well that consists of an alcoholic beverage of some sort; most likely beer or straight whiskey. Black Coffee also grows a full beard overnight. This is especially impressive if Black Coffee is a female.

THE SUGAR FREE NONFAT LATTE

The Sugar Free Nonfat Latte shows up in gym clothes to order their drink. At least 40% of the time they are actually participating in a gym-like activity on that day. They have an honest intention to be healthier and consume healthier but their life is so damn hectic. Their day is a balancing act of grocery shopping, texting, and finding an excuse to go to Target. Sugar Free Nonfat Lattes take comfort in knowing that their daily Green Straw fix provides the caffeine high needed to function at cocaine capacity. Spending over $5 a day on a daily beverage is completely justified and worth every penny because they have a litter of children at home and this is the only way to maintain sanity. Plus the cup doubles as a stress release when they clutch it in frustration. If the Sugar Free Nonfat Latte is wearing a hat it means they did not wash their hair. The Sugar Free Nonfat Latte is a high maintenance mate but is goal oriented and means well. They are often times burdened with acting busier than they really are and suffer from being easily overwhelmed. This is managed with an excessive use of whiteboards and to-do lists. They are the most fun as a drinking buddy because they *really* know how to let loose and have a mouth dirtier than a drunken marine.

THE SOY CHAI LATTE

The Soy Chai Latte is a modern day hippie. Not a real true hippie because those people are drinking at the local coffee shop and scoffing at corporate slave drivers. They order soy because they claim to be lactose intolerant. They're not. It makes them feel sophisticated and advanced to order soy and snub their nose at the people ordering the puss-tainted cow juice. Sheep. The Soy Chai Latte reads blogs and possibly writes one as well. They probably take pictures of themselves at the coffee shop or the foam on their latte and post them on all of the social media platforms with all sorts of fancy filters and hash tags. **#soy #coffeeart #ithinkiamuniquebutiamnot.** They are probably wearing some sort of scarf or an excessive amount of layers for the current weather. The Soy Chai Latte loves the free wifi at the coffee shop and surfs the net on their Mac; which is covered with insignia proclaiming their stance as a Liberal American. The Soy Chai Latte is a great mate as they are deeply sensitive and loving. They are also cat lovers and live a very frugal lifestyle. They dream of traveling the world to places like Oregon and Washington. Mates of the Soy Chai Latte: Beware! When you get to the intimacy game and come rounding the bases and sliding into home, don't be alarmed as they probably don't shave upstairs or downstairs. Au natural! It is all forgiven as they serenade you on their acoustic guitar or flute.

THE ESPRESSO

Well hel-lo! The Espresso is sophisticated and well traveled and all of us should be impressed by their worldly knowledge and the massive amounts of leather bound books in their library. If the Espresso is a man, they wear blue jeans with belts and their shirt tucked in and they likely carry a man purse. If the Espresso is a woman, they are one of two things. They are either foreign and visiting the states or they are American and so fucking tired they are shooting the espresso like good tequila to catch a quick buzz without the guilt of using cocaine. The Espresso is insulted when people call their drink "EX-presso" and look down on them with disgust. They are into the arts and enjoy a fine wine. The Espresso wears Aviator sunglasses and uses winking as a form of communication. The Espresso is a good mate but is very selective and tends to make their mate feel inferior. An Espresso is best matched with another Espresso. They are the only person who will understand their taste for the finer things in life. They will live happily ever after with no children and traveling the world while flying first class and reading books written by dead people.

THE CARMEL FRAPPIE
The Frappie. Oh, the adorable Frappie. We were all a Frappie once but then we went through puberty. However, some people never quite grow up enough to enjoy the real flavor of coffee and those are the Carmel Frappies. They hate the taste of coffee but they sure do love ice cream and they like getting high on caffeine so they order the sugar blended drink and indulge in brain freeze after brain freeze. Calories are of no concern and they usually stand in front of the pastry case trying to decide whether the cinnamon roll or the espresso brownie sounds good for lunch. The Frappie loves to party. They are probably high or hung-over when ordering the drink. They have probably been praised for their ability to do a keg stand. They do what they want. The Frappies life motto is YOLO. They usually come and order the drink right before work, making them late for their shift but they don't give a shit. The Frappie is really fun to date but they won't put a ring on it; that is unless you are willing to wait around until they are about 34. By that time they are a Black Coffee anyways.

THE TWO PUMP SUGAR FREE VANILLA NONFAT NO FOAM ONE AND A HALF SPLENDA EXTRA HOT LATTE
Douche bag. You've been warned.

I am a schizophrenic when it comes to my coffee order. My drink is determined by many factors including weather, menstrual cycle, bank account, how recently I brushed my teeth and my kid's behavior that morning. It is no coincidence that my coffee order has a direct correlation to my mood. Those closest to me know that they just need to look at my drink to determine which Jennie they are dealing with that day. The man I fell in love with ended up being the BLACK COFFEE. His stability is the perfect complement to my erratic nature. Fuck those dating websites. Everything you need to know is encrypted in your daily coffee fix.

When I Grow Up...

"Miss Jennifer. What do you want to be when you grow up?" I was already annoyed. I didn't want to grow up. I was having a good time in this whole kid jig. Why would I want to end this wild experience of macaroni, My Little Pony and labeled underpants? This bitch must be crazy. I will appease her and reply with a cliché answer. Maybe the old "nurse" or "teacher" answer will get her off my adolescent back. If anyone in their right damn mind can declare what they want to be when they grow up BEFORE the age of 22, I don't trust them. They are either over-ambitious or delusional and I personally don't find it healthy to associate with either.

Here I am at the ripe age of 32 and I have finally figured it out. Crazy, right? I know. Perhaps the caffeine accelerated my discovery. It might have been the beer. Nonetheless, I have solved the riddle that is life and found some helpful clues along the way. I will share one little clue that came in the form of an ancient artifact. This artifact from my past held valuable signs and hints about my future. I simply needed to put it all together, like an algebra equation or Wheel of Fortune puzzle. When studied, this tool can be a magic formula. It can be a compass. It can also be absolutely worthless but it is a hell of a lot of fun so there is that... And here it is...

Close your eyes. Imagine you're in a dark room that smells of new wood furniture. Why? I don't know, but I want to make sure we are all in the same place. The temperature is a balmy 73 degrees and it is probably around 2:13 in the afternoon. You can hear my voice approaching in the distance. I am running towards your dark room with a piece of paper that is illuminated and I am screaming at the top of my lungs. As I arrive in your dark box of emotion, I am so out of breath with excitement that it takes me a moment to share the good news. You can barely contain the anticipation as you await the words that are about to come out of my mouth and change the course of your life forever. The paper is so bright that it lights up the whole room like a torch. "I have discovered the answer to your destiny." *Bible*? No. *Personality test*? No. The expression on your face goes from deep and genuine curiosity to annoyance and disgust. What could I possibly possess in my left hand that would create such excitement and enthusiasm? The answer? A high school yearbook.

Yep. Many of life's holy answers can be found in your high school yearbook, along with a few potential comedy sketches. Before you begin to profusely thank me for my imparted wisdom, I will say "you're welcome." For I am about to share with you how your high school yearbook can become the road map to your future. Hear me out.

Buried deep in the pages of your yearbook are the hieroglyphics of life; the ancient markings of your future. They are found on the front pages, the back pages, and everywhere and anywhere in between. When overanalyzed, the messages your peers left you as you departed the land of high school are the tarot cards of life. What many have failed to discover is THIS is where the golden nuggets of destiny lie. Let me elaborate.

It wasn't until I was moving my younger sister out of our parent's house and into her new home of sin with her boyfriend that I became aware of this phenomenon. I was packing her yearbooks and I started to get snoopy. This is pretty typical behavior of an older sister and even more typical of a helicopter sister like me. I was flipping through the pages in hopes of finding something juicy or some old high school gossip as ammunition to harass her. As I read across the pages, I quickly noticed a pattern. This blatant pattern caused me to become slightly annoyed. Every single person who had signed the pages of that yearbook was fawning over my sister and how "beautiful" she was and how "nice" she was and how "amazing" she was as a person. Okay, fair enough. This was all true, but to see that hundreds of people all shared this adoration for my sister was strange. Like the entire student body had come to a consensus that this is how they saw Amanda Kristen. *Beautiful and nice.*

Before I could even finish packing the yearbook, I began searching for my yearbook like a frantic nut job. I was throwing around trophies and photo albums in the closet under the stairs as though the cure for cancer was under one of those boxes. I found them carelessly buried under a box of tax documents. All four of my high school yearbooks, now 10-13 years old, sat in a box of holy treasure. I dusted them off and stared at them like I was about to view Holy Scripture.

As I slowly opened my senior yearbook, I started scanning across the multi-colored autographs. I began to read each and every signature inside the cover. My adorable excitement quickly melted away. I began to realize that my signatures were much different than those I had read in my sister's yearbook. I am well aware that my sister and I are opposites of polar distinction, but seeing it on holy paper such as a yearbook can be a brutal experience. Right away I saw a pattern. They all vary in legibility and punctuation, but they all share the same common theme. *I was a hysterically inappropriate wild child.* Below is a signature from someone named Tara that sums up nearly every farewell in my yearbook:

"Jenny. You are so hysterical. Remember when we ditched 3rd and totally got caught. HAHAHA! Hope to see you next year. Good luck with Tim."

This was literally every signature in my yearbook written 67 different ways. I look at this farewell from Tara from 2001 and I see so many innuendos and clues. How the hell did I miss this? First, this bitch spelled my name wrong. I can tell you that I was a friend collector. I had many good friends, but not a lot of great friends. Hence, nobody knew me well enough to know I spell my name with a fucking IE. Everyone knows a great friend spells your goddamn name right. What I can take away from this simple misspelling is that I am the same friend-collecting loner that I was thirteen years ago. That's just who I am and I own it. I prefer to have many people that I keep at an arms distance and one really great friend than have it the other way around.

Second clue: I was "hysterical." Apparently, this is the first and most important trait that someone recognizes in me. At least 90% of my yearbook signings mentioned my humor. There was no mention of my looks or my academics. I actually didn't even know that I was funny in high school. Had I realized this, I would have known that I should never do anything where I need to be taken seriously. I should've embraced my dominating trait and owned it like a fucking hot rod. My experience with yearbook code deciphering has taught me that there is always a theme. Whether it is academic, athletics, humor, good looks, or party habits, the public comes to a general consensus right there on the pages of your yearbook. Your dominating trait is part of your own personal brand. It is a defining aspect of your character. Learn to use this to your advantage.

Tara then talks about when we ditched 3rd period and got caught. This is an absolutely true story. I thought I would awake the sleeping rebel inside of me and ditch Math and possibly choke on some cigarettes outside the school gates. Watch out world. About 3 yards from the school exit, an overweight security guard catches me. Mind you, I am a very studious and academic Senior in high school. As I am getting caught committing a rather menial crime and being escorted to the detention hall, I glance outside the school gates at all the douche bags who successfully made it through the chain link fence to the outside world. Wow. Embarrassing. Those who had escaped could barely dress themselves and yet they masterminded the trenches of our school attendance police. Needless to say, I could scratch criminal off my list of potential occupations. I still suck at breaking rules and often turn myself in before I can even commit a crime. I like to think of myself as a rebel, but let's keep it real: *Safety* is my middle name.

"Hope to see you next year." Here in lies my extreme need for comfort and routine. I did NOT go away for school. I could have gone to *almost* any college and I chose a college three miles from my front door. I was content in Oceanside. I could not leave my family. I did not want to explore or expand. I liked feeling safe. Still true today as evident by my lack of worldly travel and the tether on my ankle that prevents me from exploring anything outside my bubble. Adventure is out there, but I am not interested.

Finally, "Good luck with Tom." I was a long term dater. I spent much of high school with the same dude. I was more known as "Jennie and Tom" than I was known as just Jennie. Even after Tom, I *always* had a boyfriend. Independence was a foreign concept. I was not a "SINGLE and ready to MINGLE" kind of girl. I was a hopeless romantic. I loved being in love. From the moment I graduated I knew I wanted to be married with children as soon as possible. And all of this proved true when I fell in love, got pregnant and married at the age of 23. One thing that has changed is I am now a fully functioning independent woman. Independence was a character trait that I had to painfully learn along my journey.

WOW!! All of that from a fucking yearbook signature?! You bet your bottom dollar. Deciphering the yearbook code is a beautiful art and a great exercise of looking at yourself through the eyes of your peers. It is also beneficial to reflect on who you were as a teenager. It is great to recognize your character. Your character is all of the special things about yourself that stay the same no matter the circumstance and no matter your age. It is your character that calls the shots during life's pivotal moments. I would never suggest that you should change anything about yourself because of how people perceive you, but it is always good to know what people see when they are with you. They might see something that you don't. Put it in your journal and file it under "good to know."

Allow me to demonstrate the deciphering with some yearbook excerpts of other folks we all know from our high school years...

"Wes. Dude. You r fucking nuts. I still can't believe the shit you pulled at GPA. Can't wait to party and go to the desert." – T-Nuts

Let us laugh in chorus before we even move on because you and I both know what is coming. This is because we all knew a "Wes" in High School. Some of us used to be the Wes. I am pretty sure I dated a "Wes" in High School; probably because I wanted to "change" him. Let's begin. Note that there is no mention of school or scholarly activity. Wes probably isn't a star student and a residency is not something in Wesley's near future. This is not because Wes is not smart. He is probably a genius who can't figure out what to do with all the brains in him there head. His friends communicate with each other like single-celled douche tools. The signee then goes on to note how "nuts" he is. His mother must be proud and perpetually stressed out. As yearbook deciphering has taught me, being "nuts" is loosely translated as risky, daring and lacking noodles. He also was probably a little bit of a showboat. As an adult, how do you capitalize on these traits? How do these traits translate as one ages? Truth is there are very few options. One path might be professional athlete or something of that nature. Another path is a mediocre occupation made manageable by a raging nightlife that carries on way too long and far too often. You already know the character I am talking about. However, I will give credit where credit is due. I applaud the person who can turn a partying habit into a paying occupation. You know. The clubber who becomes a DJ. The stoner who becomes a chef. The graffiti artist who goes on to become a graphic designer. Big ups. They mastered the biggest challenge we face in life; turning a passion into a career. This is what we hope for Wes. Unfortunately, I am friends with a "Wes" on Facebook and I will spoil the surprise and tell you he didn't. He should have referred to his yearbook signatures and had some reflection time. Being "nuts" is a size we must outgrow. It doesn't look good on a grown ass man.

"Erin, I enjoyed sitting next to you in AP Calc. Ms Brown was sooooo boring! Thanks for car-pooling with me in water polo. Good luck at NYU next year."

Ahhh…squeaky clean Erin. Go ahead and be annoyed with her over-achieving and studious persona. Just know she is the one having the last laugh right now. She went hard all through high school and it is paying off. She probably went to school three times longer than the average person and graduated with 17 more degrees. She most likely works at a job with a salary with two commas and to top it off she is probably happy. *Classy bitch.* She went to school on the other side of the country to gain culture and experience, while I played beer pong in a garage in my hometown. She played high school water polo but not because she was passionate about throwing a ball while narrowly avoiding drowning, but because she knew it would look good on her college applications. She was a planner. Erin had her shit together at the ripe age of 17 and still kicks ass at life. Well played Erin.

"Erica, Call me sometime this summer. Let's get some MHL and hang out. –Luke"

MHL is a girly alcoholic beverage. Erica was a whore, or at least Luke was hoping the rumors were true.

While we all grow and mutate and change from that awkward little worm we were in high school, it is still a pretty consistent indicator of who we become as adult butterflies. High school sets a tone for how the next decade of our life plays out, good or bad. It is the first set of steps in your journey. If you want to know who you were as a person during this hormonal time, refer to your yearbook. You will find a theme and you will see a pattern. Most definitely, you will notice these themes and patterns carried on into your twenties and so on. Take those signatures serious.

And don't worry – I didn't forget about all you folks who don't have yearbooks. You didn't give a fuck back then and you probably still have zero fucks to give. I dig that. Laid back. Easy going. Solid.

In Closing...

In the spirit of full disclosure, I should tell you that I am not a Doctor. I am not a Psychiatrist. Shit, I don't even have a college degree. I don't have trophies or medals and my resume is nothing to admire. I have not experienced a miracle or accomplished some extraordinary fete. I am just a normal human being walking a normal path each and every normal day.

I am simply trying to be the best fucking version of me that I can possibly be. Most of this book is potty-mouthed story telling of my experiences along the way. I find that stories are best told with colorful language and sassy undertones. It is my hope that there are other normal people out there who will relate and enjoy this shit.

When we experience challenges or hurdles in life, we don't always need deep and dark insightful moments. We don't always need profound self-discovery and enlightenment. Sometimes we just need basic advice and relatable moments, followed by a hug and a beer. Think of this book as a conversation with your sister. Or think of it as a therapy session but the therapist is piss drunk.

If nothing else, I hope you are entertained. Now go put on some red lipstick and be the classy bitch that you are...XOXO

Made in the USA
Columbia, SC
30 November 2018